Praise for Vicki Iovine's
Girlfriends' Guides . . .

The Girlfriends' Guide to Getting Your Groove Back

"With an engaging mix of humor, firsthand experience and the insights of other girlfriends, she urges women to relish this phase of motherhood (and their independence from diaper bags), while also realizing that they can't turn the clock back."   —*Publishers Weekly*

The Girlfriends' Guide to Toddlers

"Chatty, hilarious, informative and wise . . . Iovine offers the kind of frank, sanity-saving advice you might get from a beloved best friend who's already been there."   —*Bookpage*

"Iovine and the Girlfriends are back at it again, granting us the benefit of their considerable experience on everything toddlerish."
—*The Austin Chronicle*

"Well-written and graced with humor, *The Girlfriends' Guide* will, like a good friend, help get you through those first wobbly years of motherhood."   —*Chicago Tribune*

"Iovine offers entertaining anecdotes and sage advice on raising kids from ages one to three . . . this seasoned mom knowledgeably walks readers through the toddler trenches . . . fans will be delighted in this latest volume in the *Girlfriends'* series, and new mothers warily approaching their child's toddlerhood will find that Iovine's take on these challenging years is as reasonable as that of any 'expert'—and quite a bit funnier."   —*Publishers Weekly*

continued on next page . . .

Also by Vicki Iovine

THE GIRLFRIENDS' GUIDE TO PREGNANCY

THE GIRLFRIENDS' GUIDE TO PREGNANCY DAILY DIARY

THE GIRLFRIENDS' GUIDE TO SURVIVING THE FIRST YEAR OF MOTHERHOOD

THE GIRLFRIENDS' GUIDE TO TODDLERS

THE GIRLFRIENDS' GUIDE TO GETTING YOUR GROOVE BACK

THE GIRLFRIENDS' GUIDE TO BABY GEAR

(with Peg Rosen)

The Girlfriends' Guide to Parties and Playdates

Conquer the chaos . . . and have some fun while you're at it!

Vicki Iovine

with Peg Rosen

A Perigee Book

Some of the Girlfriends' names have been changed to protect their privacy . . .
but Girlfriends, you know who you are.

A Perigee Book
Published by The Berkley Publishing Group
A division of Penguin Putnam Inc.
375 Hudson Street
New York, New York 10014

First edition: January 2003

Visit our website at www.penguinputnam.com

This book has been catalogued with The Library of Congress.

Printed in the United States of America

10   9   8   7   6   5   4   3   2   1

Contents

Contents

Part 2: Parties: The Mother of All Fun Occasions

Acknowledgments

Finally. The work, late nights, whining, nit-picking, obsessing and heated debate about all things playful are over, and here is the end result. An honest-to-goodness book. Really and truly, it has been a collaborative effort, and there are many thanks to give.

Vicki Iovine, thank you so much for your friendship through these many years and for the amazing opportunities you have sent my way. You are a Girlfriend with a capital G and one heck of an inspiration. Thanks, Christine Pepe, for your support and encouragement over all of these months. You're not only a terrific editor but a great therapist.

Thanks goes to the many professionals who came to the plate when I asked them to help with this book. Key among them are Claire Lerner, L.C.S.W., Child Development Specialist, Zero to Three; and Stanley Greenspan, M.D., clinical professor of psychiatry, behavioral science, and pediatrics at George Washington University Medical School.

Acknowledgments

Then, of course, there are the Girlfriends whose advice and real, live birthday party and playdate experiences are at the heart of this book. Bianca Bator, Judy Sciarra, and Jamie Scurletis—I love you and owe you big time for fielding all those late-night and early-morning interrogations about virtually every aspect of your maternal existence. Thanks also to Georgia Scurletis, Gail Belsky, Cathy Meier Asher, Jill Stein, Kate Kelly, Jeannie Rosen, Lauren Picker, Alma Schneider-Saltzman, Nancy Mattia, Holly Robinson, Mary Beth Rosenthal, and Connie Fowler for your willingness to play along. As for the dozens and dozens of other amazing Girlfriends who have participated in my Motherhood Network over the past years, I am indebted to you for sharing your stories, your wisdom, and your time. You serve as a constant reminder of how the bond of motherhood really can bring people from all walks of life together.

Thanks to my mother and dad, Carol and Bob Rosen, for showing me firsthand how much fun childhood and parenthood can be. A huge thanks as well to Florence Freundlich. If someone had told me that my mother-in-law would turn out to be one of my very best Girlfriends, I'd have said they were crazy. Consider it—and the fact that this job got done—as proof that anything is possible. Gabi—this has been one crazy year. Thanks so much for hanging in there and keeping everyone happy. We'll miss you.

Finally, thank you, thank you, to the three most important individuals in my life. They are not Girlfriends; they are, in fact, 100 percent male: my dear husband, Paul, and my sons, Ben and Noah. Together, the three of you are my heart, my breath, the very meaning of my life. I love you "to the moon and back."

Why We Wrote This Book

The Party Truth

I am the Yoda (with much, much better jewelry) of children's parties and playdates. You know me well enough to realize that I don't normally delude myself about my mothering prowess, but this is just undeniable; ask anybody who knows me. Peg is definitely a Jedi Master, but her age and relative inexperience will forever keep her looking up to me for the secrets of the Social Force. By the time this guide reaches your bookstore, I will have thrown forty-eight birthday parties for kids!

Just let that concept sink in a moment. I have four kids between the ages of nine and fifteen and heaven forbid any one of them should be feted any less fabulously than his or her siblings. This is particularly nerve-racking because three of my kids have birthdays within four weeks of each other, so they have all the details memorized and can tell you who had more confetti, better entertainment, or a funnier cake.

And if I've hosted forty-eight parties, I must have attended four hundred eighty. You'll soon learn, if you haven't already, that reciprocity is a critical part of being a successful party thrower. As I tell my own lazy kids, if they don't suit up and show up for their friends' early-Saturday-morning paint ball parties, then they better not be disappointed when those friends don't show up for their own karaoke/hula lesson party.

One thing I've discovered over the years is that I actually *love* parties and playdates. I love the way they start as a concept, the way the kids and I collaborate on the ideal party and how to bring it into the realm of reality. I even find addressing the invitations therapeutic. Of course, I work from the home and have writing projects lined up from here till Tuesday, so the mindless act of using my cutest cursive to copy addresses onto envelopes is the second-best thing I can think of to do in bed at night. And, if you do the first thing first, it should only set you back about ten minutes and you will be in the perfect Zen state to complete envelopes for all the girls/boys in your little darling's third-grade class.

When RSVPs start coming in, however, I'm as aggressive as a pit bull. As we suggest later in this book, no invitation should be sent without a drop-dead date for RSVPs. That won't inspire that last third of the parents to put their party manners on, but it will give you complete etiquette entitlement to call them and torment their voice mail until they commit or decline. I like that part, too, even though there are the occasional heartbreaks when a best friend will be out of town or, God forbid, another child has scheduled a party for the same day (don't spend too much time worrying about that because we provide recommendations for clearing a calendar and saving dates for our precious birthday boys and girls).

Jimmy, my husband, swears I always overcaffeinate the morning of a child's party. I confess, it's true. When I look back at the photos and videos (which have all been transferred to DVD—more about that later, too), I look about ready to jump into the cake or about to tackle Barney. I run around micromanaging the party like a Border collie keeping her lambs under her paw.

I apologize for nothing, not one hysterical moment, not one extra trip to Starbucks, and here's why: Birthday parties are like fine wine. They ripen and burnish with the passage of time. To tell you the honest truth, few mothers say good-bye to their last little guest and sit back to congratulate themselves on the social event of the semester. I run straight for the wine and say a silent prayer of thanks that we all survived and nothing truly horrible happened (except when something truly horrible has happened).

Children's memories are somewhat sketchy up to the age of six or seven. Don't let their ability to dial Grandma's house alone at age five fool you—their brains are like little colanders, holding and letting slip equally precious and well-intentioned memories like the nonsense about how their name was spelled wrong on their balloons or if Daddy talked on the phone too much during the party. Let Yoda tell you something that you can take to the bank. You may think that your child's genius brain is like a sponge, but that's just not true. I can prove it by inviting you to come to my house to watch old birthday party videos with my kids. *What they remember is what we intend for them to remember.* If we edit out the part where they hated the pet ferret who came to the third birthday party, they forget the ferret. If we show all the smiles and friends and loving relatives and gifts, that's how they perceive the entire event.

What is the lesson we learn here? That your job is to sacrifice yourself as much as you can to the red-letter days, get on video participating in the hula hoop contest, do lots of close-ups of your child being sung to and blowing out the candles and spend a lot of film on the sheer adorableness of the birthday child. My ten-year-old son recently watched himself as a toddler on video gleefully pulling all the tissue paper out of a box and spreading it across the kitchen island and was enchanted with how adorable he was.

Dress silly, be fun, "be here now" at the party (don't even think of trying to accomplish anything else except maybe one potty visit for you and the celebrant), let the unexpected happen (like the infamous Iovine Cake Face Dunk) and play happy, peppy music in the background. The proof of the pudding doesn't really come for another three or four years.

"Oh, sure," you may be muttering, "what about all the moms at kindergarten coffee who will weigh in like Dominick Dunne about whether the party was a success?" Won't happen, Girlfriend. Moms only talk about really crummy, pathetic parties (which this guide ensures against) or about the freaky ones that either look like the parents spent the kid's college tuition on the event, or like the nanny was the only person who knew all the children's names while the mother sat in a corner looking terrified of the guests and their parents and anyone else who walked into the room, or worst of all, about the parties where it looked like the kids' happiness and safety were not properly ensured.

As for Playdates . . .

It has long been my secret yearning to be the most popular mother around. Whether I've achieved this private goal is still not clear, but I'm committed to trying until my kids no longer live here or even come home for the holidays. I really like my kids' friends, especially now that we're out of the hitting and biting stage, but more important, I'd rather have all the kids here trying to get into mischief than at someone else's house. Maybe I'm delusional, but I think I'm particularly energetic and, thanks to an ill-spent youth, exceptionally wise to the tricks and temptations of young people. Since I already have four kids, adding another three or four each weekend for sleepovers or for after-school playdates isn't that much of a life change for me. Then again, I do think it's caused early-onset senility in me and that's why I'm so glad to be writing with my Girlfriend, Peg—she's younger and in the thick of the party/playdate road race.

Peg, the mother of little boys, is right beside me, keeping me current and preventing the veil of sentimentality from falling across my eyes. Our Girlfriend/Editor/Muse, Chris, is the mother of two little girls. Like the Donny and Marie song goes, "They're a little bit East Coast, I'm a little bit L and A." Together, we represent a wide range of demographics: families who live in apartments, families who must drive long distances to parties, families who don't expect to celebrate out of doors after Halloween and families who plan pool parties for January birthdays, families who live within spitting distance of every toy store and fast-food restaurant advertised during Saturday morning TV and families who save all major shopping for a drive to another county once a week and otherwise rely on the Internet and catalogs.

Oh yeah, one more interesting thing: I feel like I'm validated once more as the Yoda of Parties and Playdates because I have two boys and two girls; I know the ins and outs of a pink hair–extension party as well as I know how important a mouth-guard is for a Punt, Pass, and Kick party.

Relax and take a deep breath, Girlfriend. Peg, Chris, all the Original Girlfriends, and a whole bunch of new friends you're just going to adore are all here for you. These social obligations will not only be manageable for you, they'll be terrific memories. Just have faith; have we ever misled you yet? *Let's get ready to party!*

Introduction: The Road to Hell Is Paved with Good Intentions

It's my party and I'll cry if I want to.

Picture this: Vicki is the first mother in her children's school to have the divine inspiration to hold her son's kindergarten-age party at a brand-new, totally hip kid's play club. Not only does it feature the best music on a state-of-the-art system, it is decorated in colors she would consider wearing! There are forty-two guests because every classmate in every kindergarten class has been invited. The children are absolutely adorable, the staff is competent and copious, and Vicki's husband, for what it's worth regarding this incident, is present and draped with cameras. Other familiar faces include her mother-in-law and several of her Original Gs (the Malibu Girlfriends from the early guides to pregnancy and toddlers). After a couple of get-to-know-ya games, the kids are released to the maze of slides, tunnels, and rope ladders. Within seven minutes, darling little Robbie, twin brother of Rochelle, bravely hops up to await his turn on the infamous Zip Line. His predecessor throws it with all his might to make sure it makes it to Robbie's side without needing grown-up assistance.

Oh, it makes it, all right, not only close enough for Robbie to grab it but with enough heft that the metal triangle collides with Robbie's forehead. Vicki, who has a nose for mayhem, is right there beside Robbie when it happens. First there's just a white mark across his brow, but she knows what's coming. The blood fills in the shape of a triangle and then begins pouring down Robbie's face. He was so sweet—he didn't cry a tear—as Vicki carried him down the rope ladder (who knows how?) and into the bathroom for a water wash and some bright light. That may have been her Waterloo. Seeing a child's flesh opened on your watch is one of the worst feelings a mom can experience. The only thing that kept Vicki from fainting dead away was her awareness that head wounds bleed more than a cow slaughter even when the damage is minimal.

Robbie, ever cooperative, walks out with Vicki to find his "escort," who happens to be his grandma, because mom and dad are enjoying a rare weekend out of town. Now what to do? Does Vicki leave her son and his siblings and the forty-odd kids at the party place to take Robbie to the hospital? Does he even really need a hospital? If Vicki were his mom, what would Vicki expect the party mom to do? Why, oh why did Vicki opt not to serve beer and wine for the parents? Oh yeah, she learned that lesson years ago.

Grandma was the voice of reason, reassuring Vicki that she and Gramps would take Robbie to the doctor to see if he needed stitches and that Vicki belonged at the party to make sure the forty other kids didn't get injured, too. Vicki still sees Robbie in fifth grade and can still make out the scar on his forehead, which makes her want to weep. His parents were so kind and forgiving (perhaps because they had several other kids), but Vicki will feel beholden to them till her dying day.

The Bermuda Triangle Playdate

Girlfriend Shelli hosts a playdate for her daughter Jody and her two best friends from preschool, Cindy and Laura. Shelli picks up all the girls in car pool, dutifully rounding up the girls' car seats and struggling to install them in her SUV. Everyone wants to sit next to the star of the playdate, Jody, so Shelli has to move her own daughter's car seat to the middle of the passenger bench and diplomatically place Cindy and Laura on either side. Naturally, one of the seat belt buckles is buried somewhere and although the temptation runs high, Shelli's higher self forces her to pull out of the car pool lane and into the open parking lot to lift the entire SUV seat in search of it. All the while she is cursing the car wash guys who are the only other people who ever lift the heavy middle seat.

As she breaks her middle nail to the quick, Shelli lifts the seat and finds the buckle, as well as a missing thermometer, her two midsized hot rollers, and two Flinstones vitamins. Never, ever, does she stop smiling and building up the fun they're going to have. Heaven forbid that little Cindy or Laura should go home and report that Jody's mom is "mean" or "grouchy."

Within an hour of returning home, Cindy is whining because she thinks Jody and Laura play more with each other than with her and they don't like her as much. Everything would be fine if only Cindy can call her mom and tell on all of you. Shelli, being human, tells Cindy that the phones aren't working right now, but that she'll give her the necklace of her choice from Shelli's jewelry box to show her that she really is loved by everyone there.

Shelli goes upstairs in search of costume jewelry and comes down to find Laura and Jody playing Chutes and Ladders and no sign of Cindy. When the other girls are asked where the third point in their triangular playdate is, they vacantly say, "She's in Jody's room picking out her favorite Barbie." Thirty minutes later, when Shelli checks back in with her little angels, she gets the same answer about Cindy—not a good sign. In that instant, Shelli loses about 20,000 miles off her motherhood treads and streaks from room to room begging Cindy to come out, come out, wherever she is. No response.

What to do next? Call Cindy's mother weeping and break it to her that her beloved child has been misplaced while in Shelli's care? Downplay the crisis and call another mother who knows Cindy and might have some sensitive insight about how to tell the mother that her child is gone? No, Shelli throws herself onto the carpet in the family room and has a nervous breakdown in front of her daughter and Laura, who are just now looking up from Chutes and Ladders. "Oh, girls, if you don't help me search every inch of this house right now to find Cindy, I'm going to get one of my horrible migraines," she wails.

"She's in my closet," says Jody flatly. "She always goes in my closet when her feelings are hurt." Who should Shelli throttle at this point, her nonplussed daughter or the drama queen who has been lying among Jody's shoes and ignoring Shelli's pathetic calls?

The Excedrin Family Outing

It's Vicki's turn again, poor dear. Summer is drawing to a close and the kids have completed sports camps, drama classes, and remedial spelling. All eyes turn to Mom for some fun, some adventure, something worthy of the scrapbooks they someday intend to create together. Aha, thinks Vicki, as she reads the leisure section of the *Los Angeles Times*. Catalina Island is just "26 miles across the sea" and it's "waitin' for me." It's such an easy trip now on the hovercraft boats; Vicki, her four kids and two of their dearest friends can be there in an hour.

Well, it's a little overcast and chilly for kayaking and snorkeling. They walk back to the harbor to get in line for the glass-bottom boat. Naturally, there is one adult and six small children, and the two youngest don't want to get on the boat in case a shark comes. Okay, this is fine. The boat never moves more than fifty yards from the dock so Vicki can keep it within her peripheral vision while she takes the two five-year-olds over to the lady who sells frozen bananas.

By the time the big kids come back from their ocean adventure, Vicki and the little ones have pretty much had their fill of Catalina. Oops, we forgot about the other four kids who've worked up quite an appetite at sea. "Why do they get frozen bananas and we don't?" they respectfully query. By the time all bananas are bought and then thrown in the trash for not having enough chocolate and nuts on them, it's 11:45 A.M. No problem. Vicki is holding return tickets to San Pedro Harbor at 4:00 P.M. Let's see, they can rent one golf cart (no cars are allowed on the island) and five kids can stand beside the road while Vicki gives each one a ride.

Or, how about this great indigenous cactus museum that the tour books all say just can't be missed? Vicki, God bless her, buys seven tickets for this encounter with nature at its prickliest. The older kids give her the benefit of the doubt but start laughing the minute they begin reading the self-guided tour. The littler ones, much quicker to recognize a con than their elders, begin crying immediately. Vicki deliriously believes that Catalina is morphing into Alcatraz right before her very eyes.

Supermom!

After a ten-hour workday, Margot is welcomed home by her son, Ben, who is just begging to play pretend garage. Margot is dying to go to the bathroom and knows if she doesn't return a particular call tonight, she will be considered permanently MIA. Still, she is willing to test her bladder and put the phone call out of her mind for sweet Ben. She gets down on the floor with her mini-mechanic and makes convincing *vrooom, vroooom* noises. "These tires need to be rotated," she announces in her best pit voice. "And we need to do lots of lubing here, Ben Boy, so start at the front and work your way back," she decrees, hoping to buy some time to take off her panty hose and put her hair up in a scrunchie. She's so good. She's hanging in there as if she were a NASCAR tailgater. She can practically smell the delicious combination of gasoline and barbecue. Oh, look, there's Ashley Judd and the Dixie Chicks serving up the hot dogs . . . oops, Margot is dreaming after having been asleep for who knows how long? Where's Ben!! She wipes the drool from her face and jumps up from the floor with enough energy to burst a hole in the wall. Ben's fine; he's found her hidden black Sharpie and has retreated to his bedroom to write the alphabet, what he can remember of it, on the walls.

Are We Having Fun Yet?

Aw shucks, we don't mean to scare you right from the opening pages. To tell you the truth, we suspect that you've either imagined equally terrifying social encounters with your tots or actually experienced something like them. It's the stone-cold truth: Deep inside the heart of many loving, devoted, passionately involved and hopelessly dedicated mommies of young children, there is a virtually unutterable secret. Okay, there are probably a few, but for our own purposes, the Girlfriends are going to focus in on one in particular: When push comes to shove, "having fun" with little kids can be, well . . . almost impossible.

The simple fact that you have picked up this book tells us that you are a devoted parent and you want to share the joys o' life with your children. With that essential truth about you duly acknowledged, let us give you this first piece of Girlfriendly advice:

Cut yourself some slack!

In case no one has pointed this out to you already, having young children is an all-consuming endeavor. If you're anything like us, practically every move you make—however indirect it may be—is somehow related to ensuring your family's well-being.

That includes staying late at the office on a Wednesday night so you won't have to work over the weekend, or parking your preschooler in front of Nickelodeon for an hour so you can attack that enormous pile of bills before the electricity (and cable!) get cut off. Granted, no one is going to giggle with delight when you take on these tasks. No one is going to tell you what a fun and happening mom you are for covering all bases. Well, no one except your Girlfriends! We have walked two moons in your mocassins and we feel as stretched and stressed as you.

Adding extra spice to our collective guilt stew are all those experts who moan about how disengaged American parents are from their children. Well, pardon us for saying so, but take a break during your next Mommy & Me class and think back to your childhood. If it was anything like ours, your mom never would have considered jumping around in public with a bunch of toddlers singing "I'm a Little Teapot." Our moms' idea of a playdate (as if the word even existed) involved the grown-ups sitting in the kitchen smoking Kools and drinking coffee while we kids played cops and robbers in the basement. A drop-off playdate basically meant shooing all humans over the age of four and under the age of eighteen out the back door and telling them not to come inside the house until supper.

Putting this down in writing makes it seem like childhood was grim (and has also offended our own mothers to no end). But for most of us, we recall that being a kid was pretty fun. Our parents drew a clear boundary between their interests and their childrens', and most of us never questioned that setup for a second. We're not laying all this out to pooh-pooh the current parenting climate or to idealize the past. The more child-focused approach that now prevails—or at least that you read about in parenting publications—can benefit everyone when it's not taken to extremes, including parents since it allows us to be a whole lot more youthful ourselves. We're just trying to provide some perspective here and to remind you how much you are already giving your child, even if in your eyes it is hardly enough.

Is Benevolent Neglect Occasionally Allowed Anymore?

The Girlfriends look back on our own experiences as newer moms and we can't believe how manic many of us were. We who worked outside the home spent what time we did have with our young children playing at a nearly frantic pace, moving from the blocks to the Barbies to God knows what, just trying to make up for the time we felt we had "missed." Those of us who stayed at home turned entertaining and enriching our babies into a profession, as if to compensate for not being "out there" earning a buck. Eventually, for most of us, playing became just another task on our to-do lists. When we were doing it, we secretly prayed for an interruption; when we weren't doing it, we felt guilty. Meanwhile, our kids simply got used to their mothers buzzing around like bees on a Starbucks high. They also got used to being spoon-fed amusement and entertainment, instead of developing the ability to find it on their own.

Then there's our Girlfriend Brett. Now the at-home mom of three kids under seven, she makes a point of spending about twenty minutes a day actually playing with her two older children. Once or twice a week, she'll agree to something they adore but she detests (like a pretend tea party); the rest of the time it's got to be something that's enjoyable for all of them (Brett and the kids all adore puzzles, for example). The rest of the day, Brett feels absolutely no compunction about leaving the older sibs up to their own devices (she permits one hour of TV in the late afternoon) or simply inviting them to help her or keep her company while she's nursing the baby, cooking, cleaning, gardening, etc. Now, you say—that's because she's an at-home mom and has the luxury of quantity time, right? Well, when Brett was working full time and had only William, her firstborn, you know how much pure play time she gave him? Only about ten minutes more than she gives her kids now. And that's primarily because she didn't have other children to attend to.

Here's her thinking, and it's what many of us eventually learned as we've had more children and as a result, less time to obsess. William did need that half hour of time devoted specifically to him and his interests. With the answering machine on and the TV and radio off, it gave Brett and her son a chance to reconnect after a long day apart. Once that one-on-one play was over, however, life went on just as if Brett had been there all day. Brett would cook while William colored at the kitchen table. She'd read her book while he paged through his own stack nearby. They had a chance to simply "be" together, without "being" in each other's faces. Call it "benevolent neglect" or the opportunity to merely bask in each other's aura—it's a relaxed, reassuring luxury that we are convinced every mom and child deserve, whether they're together all day or for only a handful of hours. The Girlfriends just think you might want to consider that point before you embark on your next guilt trip.

Maternal Fun-Making

Take our hands as we walk you through the fundamentals of what we call Maternal Fun-Making. This includes such things as Family Fun at Home, Family Outings, Other Peoples' Children Having Fun with Us, Our Children Having Fun with Other People and, ta-dah . . . the Birthday Party!!

Each of these presents its own challenges and its own wonderful opportunities, and the Girlfriends are going to help you not only survive, but perhaps occasionally enjoy them. Take our ideas, suggestions, and advice like you would select food from a smorgasbord; some things may not be to your taste and you may devour other parts (although we would suggest that before you reach for any desserts, you memorize the rules of gifting in the party section of this book. Consider it the vegetables). So, we'll start with the scene in which most childhood memories are created, the home, and we'll branch out from there.

Top Ten Worst Playdate Scenarios

10. Though the invitee is perfectly behaved, your child bites the fleshy part of his arm hard enough to bruise it. The mother is finicky and inexperienced and wants to see a copy of your child's inoculation records.

9. You try to be the Fun Mom and take the kids to McDonald's after preschool pickup to get Happy Meals. When your little visitor's father comes to pick him up, he sees the Happy Meal toy and soberly tells you, "We're raising him as a vegan."

8. You have two older kids and allow the sitter to take them, your first-grader and his playdate to a movie at the cineplex. The kids are ecstatic, but the next day the other mother calls to question your morals for letting a seven-year-old see *Austin Powers.*

7. After your child's playdate leaves, your own child comes up during dinner preparation to ask what "gay" means.

6. Your little boy comes home from a playdate, clearly distraught, and says that Mrs. So-and-So spanked him. If ever there was a time for corporal punishment for adults, this was it.

5. Your visitor arrives in a clean Pull-Up and then announces she has diarrhea. Her mother isn't home or answering her

cell and your child has been potty trained for months, making yours a diaper-free household.

4. Your chatty little visitor tells you that "Mommy is so funny at night 'cause that's when she has her martinis."

3. Your son comes home smelling like an ashtray because the other mother clearly smokes continuously, from car to house to car.

2. Your daughter returns from her playdate with a brand-new Lizzie McGuire backpack, an autographed picture, a silver bracelet, and stars in her eyes. Apparently her dad distributes for the Disney Channel. Your husband works for the local power company.

1. The mother tags along, in spite of all negotiations for this to be a drop-off playdate. You have to put on lipstick and eyebrows, not to mention a shirt less than five years old, sit down and drink coffee after your 3:00 P.M. cutoff, and sound interested in her ideas for petitioning the school for more parent hours in the preschool classroom.

Part 1

Playdates

CHAPTER ONE

The Fun House

It's a whole lot easier to have fun with your kids if your home is fun to live in. So let's talk first about setting the stage. The key to making a "fun" house has very little to do with buying out FAO Schwarz. It doesn't mean you have to resign yourself to living in a junior version of Animal House, either. The Girlfriends think a fun house is a place that makes it natural and easy for everyone in the house to spend lots of open-ended, unstructured time together. We think it's a place that's fairly organized and attractive, but is not so fussy that everyone's walking around on tiptoe. It's a place that's set up in such a way that basic materials are easily available and cleanup is a piece of cake. And it's a space that's equipped to accommodate the reality of how and where children want to spend their time. Until the age of about seven, that usually means **they want to be where we are.**

Case in point: Our Girlfriend Tricia spent a pretty large sum of money building a truly spectacular playroom on the second floor of her home for her two daughters. Floor-to-ceiling built-in shelves house hundreds of stuffed animals, oodles of Playmobil sets, an endless supply of puzzles, a bevy of Barbies, Legos upon Legos upon Legos, and the junior version of practically every board game ever invented. There's a big, cushy couch with matching tuffets, thick, cozy carpeting, and harlequin-patterned curtains draping the windows that really are to die for. The girls' bedrooms are equally elaborate and delightful.

You know where Susannah and Leah spend most of their time? Around a small plastic picnic table that Tricia plopped in the kitchen when she first moved into the house. Plunked on top of that table are wet wipes containers filled with crayons, Magic Markers, glue sticks, and a few pads of drawing paper. Underneath the table is a box filled with dress-up clothes and another chock-full of random toys dragged from elsewhere in the house. *The girls* prefer to be at the table—not because of what's on or under it—but because of who is near it. Tricia *herself* is more inclined to play with her girls in the kitchen because it's far more convenient and less of an effort for her than hauling upstairs and hunkering down to play in a mom's equivalent of domestic Siberia, especially since her cordless phone gets all crackly up there.

This all goes to say that, yes, a nice playroom or a finished basement is handy to have for playdates and birthday parties and for general horsing around. But the truth is—and really chew on this for a moment—**you'll play with your children more often and more spontaneously if they are easily able to play where you spend most of your time.**

The Kitchen

If, like Tricia, the kitchen or kitchen–great room, is your main haunt in the house, here are some basic things you can do to keep fun close at hand.

Create a Space for Your Child

Space permitting, you can, like Tricia, stick a small play table and chairs in or just outside of your kitchen. Our Girlfriend Margot—who has two boys—reserved a corner of her kitchen for a small Little Tikes play kitchen. Next to it, she parked a big picnic basket full of fake plastic food. Her oldest is going on seven at this point and that little kitchen still gets more use than any other toy in the house. Ben and Noah cook up their pretend broccoli-taco-acorn smoothies while Margot throws dinner together. They "wash" their blankies and action figures in what really is the mini-kitchen's oven. It is also what encourages the boys to stick around while mom and dad finish dinner—since it takes the kids about four seconds to eat theirs. An easel stocked with a big pad, washable Magic Markers, and crayons is another good option. If your actual kitchen happens to be only a bit bigger than a Little Tikes kitchen, you can create a sense of "special" space by keeping a waterproof blanket on hand (see sidebar on page 40) and rolling it out for your younger kids while you're in there. And just forget the idea of buying a fancy kitchen table, choose something that can take some abuse. Welcome the children to use it as their work space when it's not being used to serve your fine cuisine.

Create On-Site, Easily Accessible Toy Storage

Allowing toys in the kitchen is less of a chore if it does not require schlepping them back and forth to a far-flung toy box. Having good storage on site also decreases the likelihood that junk will end up underfoot as you're pulling a roast chicken out of the oven. There are all sorts of clever options out there, like those little benches with hidden storage under the seat. The Girlfriends think that defeats the purpose, however. First of all, with children, toys that are out of sight are essentially out of mind. (You will learn this with those big toy chests that basically become toy graveyards after a while.) Second, storage is used most when access is easy. Choose something that's open and inviting. If you're not so fancy, a laundry basket does the job just fine. If you want something prettier, pick up a big wicker basket and line it with some inexpensive fabric that complements the room. Save yourself extra running around by putting the toys away only once the basket becomes full. Come to think of it, you might want to keep one of these baskets in every room of the house where the kids are permitted to play.

Create a Basic Supply Arsenal

Half the reason why moms like us dread the idea of doing crafts projects is because of all the work that goes into setup and cleanup. You have to go to the recycling pile and pull out old newspapers. You have to hike upstairs to get smocks. You've got to scurry around looking for scissors and tape. You'll be more inclined to create cool stuff with your children or allow them to do it on their own if you have all the supplies right at your fingertips. Most of the Girlfriends have sacrificed at least one kitchen cabinet to the cause. Unlike the toy bin, we tend to keep our art supplies in a cabinet or drawer that's either lockable or out of reach so that we have control of the messier or potentially dangerous stuff (like scissors). Once your child is over the everything-goes-in-the-mouth-and-walls-are-meant-for-drawing stage, crayons, paper, and other relatively benign stuff can—and should—go right on top of the play table, if you're using one, so he'll be encouraged to dig in all on his own. When your children are a bit older still (about five or six), you can make supplies even more accessible so they can help themselves.

HERE ARE SOME KEY ITEMS TO KEEP IN YOUR KITCHEN ARSENAL:

Old newspaper—great for messy jobs; also good for collages

Old rags and towels—cleanup, cleanup

Dustbuster or similar portable, cordless vacuum

Smocks or big, junky T-shirts, for the kids and for the grown-ups

Splat mat or waterproof blanket (see a theme building here?)

Adult scissors

Child-safe scissors

Clear contact paper

Crayons

Washable markers

Construction paper

Pad of newsprint paper

Pad of paper for painting

Stickers

Craft sticks (known to regular folk as popsicle sticks)

Stamps and ink pads

Tape

Stapler

Glue sticks

Glitter sticks

Washable paints

Paintbrushes

Small- and medium-size plastic containers (to hold paint, water, etc.)

Rubber bands

Play-Doh

These things are more easily found than you'd think. Try Lakeshore Stores, craft supply stores like Michael's, catalogs, and the Internet. Your local variety store might also be a treasure trove.

Add Kid-Friendly Touches

Your goal isn't just to make it fun for your child to play in the kitchen. You want it safe for him to be in there. Along these lines we strongly recommend that you:

CHILDPROOF, CHILDPROOF, CHILDPROOF. Move really scary stuff, such as drain cleaner and food processor blades, up and entirely out of reach. Consolidate somewhat scary items, such as knives and skewers, and install childproofing devices on the drawers you keep them in. Same goes for any small objects that could present a choking hazard—check that catchall drawer with the batteries, odd screws, fridge magnets, etc. You'll be surprised by how many potentially lethal items you'll come across. Put a latch on the cabinet under the kitchen sink if you keep soaps and detergents in there. Also, change your habits. Get used to using the back burners of your stove when possible, and always turn the handles of your pots inward to reduce the risk of someone knocking into them. Put a small rug in front of the kitchen sink and stove to prevent the floor from getting wet or greasy.

INVEST IN A SMALL STEP STOOL. When your child wants to help rip up salad at the sink or wash finger paint off her hands, she'll be a lot better off if she's standing on a steady step stool instead of a chair. Your chairs will be better off, too. If you are vertically challenged, you yourself may also need the stool to reach all of those items you've put up out of reach for safety's sake. Choose a step stool with a rubberized, skidproof base so it stays put. The very best ones have a railing for the kids to hold on to, since it's so easy for them to get involved in their projects and forget that they are standing on a little square a foot or two off the ground. *Do not* invest in the adorable, wooden, personalized puzzle step stools, or anything artsy-fartsy like that. They skid like crazy and the balance can be dodgy.

BUY *BIG* MIXING BOWLS. You'll be more inclined to allow your little chef to mix the flour into the cookie batter if half the flour doesn't end up all over the kitchen counter. Big, wide bowls are much better at containing a child's enthusiastic stirring and sifting. Bowls with nonskid bottoms are particularly fabulous for kids to work with.

GIVE YOUR BABE SOME TOOLS OF THE TRADE. You'll be amazed at the incentive a child-size apron provides. Go for something fancy or pick up a blank one for a few bucks at your local hobby store and personalize it yourself with some permanent markers. Another great kitchen purchase for kids: a child-size broom. Keep it right in the broom closet with yours.

ADD MUSIC TO THE MIX. Music really does add vitality to practically any activity or chore. Keep a boom box and a stack of family-friendly CDs and tapes right on hand in the kitchen so it'll be easy to turn on tunes or stories on tape.

What Not to Keep in Your Kitchen

We think that the worst thing to keep in your kitchen or the family room that's attached to it is a television. Not just because it's pretty lame to watch TV during meals (even if you yourself aren't actually eating with your children, meals are one of your best opportunities to connect with them), but because, as the Girlfriends have learned from our own mistakes, it's just too darned easy to turn that tube on and allow *it* to entertain the babies so *we* can get our own stuff done faster. Essentially, it clobbers the opportunity for much of the creative play and interaction that can so naturally unfold when parents and children are in each other's company. Our Girlfriend Beth finally got so fed up, she moved the tube upstairs to a spare bedroom. The amazing thing was that her twins didn't follow the TV. They stayed right down in the kitchen great room and found plenty to do with Mom, with each other, and with the other fun stuff that was down there.

Since we've gone ahead and opened this can of worms, the Girlfriends are going to give you our general take on the TV issue. First and foremost, we're not anti-TV zealots. We were born and bred on Bugs Bunny and Scooby-Doo and watch our own share of *Seinfeld* and *ER* reruns whenever we have the opportunity. We're not going to lie to you, either, and tell you that we've successfully limited our children's TV-watching repertoire to public television. Once kids start any kind of school it's only a matter of time until they start flipping through the channels to find what their friends are talking about. To be fair, many children need this social currency to fit in to some extent. On evenings when we're particularly knackered, it also takes very little arm-twisting for us to give the go-ahead for extra TV or video time.

How does a mom keep the TV habit from getting out of hand? There are all kinds of strategies. Many experts recommend something called "appointment television." The idea is to sit down with your child and determine what shows she wants to watch in advance and then stick to that schedule. The Girlfriends wholeheartedly approve of the idea in concept, but find it somewhat hard to stick with. Life is darned unpredictable with young kids and there will always be unplanned occasions when, if the TV doesn't go on, mommy will simply lose her mind. Purists tell us to get rid of our TVs altogether. They're generally the same folks who want us to use and wash our own cloth diapers and compost our own potting soil. Not exactly realistic for most of us.

What's proven most helpful to us by far is one very simple concept: *Make television inconvenient.* At least while your kids are very young, forget strict schedules and rigid rules. Simply take TV out of mainstream spots like the kitchen or great room and put it in a relatively uninteresting place that requires an effort to get to—like down in the basement, off on the sunporch, or on top of Mount Everest (just kidding). If you can't move your TV out of the main living area, at least put it in a cabinet and keep it closed for most of the day. By sheer logistics, turning on the tube will become a more conscious decision, rather than a reflex—for you and your child. Things might get dicier as your child gets older and seems not at all to mind the fact that the TV is a good distance from dear old mom, but the less TV he watches now, the less intense his TV addiction will probably be down the road.

The Playroom

Those fantasy playrooms you see in the shelter magazines may look tempting, but the Girlfriends really wonder what those moms were thinking (or how much free time they had on their hands). All those fancy built-ins. All the adorable furniture. The whole point of a playroom—if you're lucky enough to have one—is to have a space where kids can let loose and raise a rumpus so they don't completely trash the rest of the house. This essentially means the more open, easy-to-clean space there is, the better. Remember, too, your kids' interests and abilities are going to change quickly as they get older and bigger. In a short time, not all storage will need to be accessible to a human who is only three feet tall. Finger-painting parties will give way to, lord help us, boy/girl get-togethers, so spending a fortune on pint-size furniture is a pretty shortsighted investment. Keep things basic and think temporary, unless of course you're gunning for a spread in *House Beautiful* or simply adore the idea of redecorating every few years. Some key points to consider:

COVER THE FLOOR: A bare floor not only gives off a chilly feel, it provides fertile ground for head bonking and other injuries. Put down some inexpensive, easy-to-clean carpeting; it adds color and warmth to the space all on its own. (Patterns and dark colors tend to hide stains best.) You might want to keep a portion bare for messy projects like painting; otherwise, just throw a big plastic tarp or shower curtain liner down when you need to. If carpeting isn't an option, buy those colorful foam tiles that fit together like a jigsaw puzzle.

REGULATE THE TEMPERATURE: Our Girlfriend Stacy's mom spent a year fixing up the family basement so the kids could have a place to play. Problem was, Stacy and her sibs hated the place because it was so darned cold and damp down there. Make sure your playroom is cozy—put in baseboard heat if you need to. (Never, ever use a space heater.) Summer isn't as big a deal, since kids tend to spend more time outside. But you might consider putting in a ceiling fan or window unit if your home isn't centrally air-conditioned.

MAKE IT SAFE: A playroom must be extra safe because it is a place where your child should be able to hang out without grown-up company (if she wants to). Make sure all unused outlets are covered. If those cheap little childproofing plugs are too easy to remove (meaning you don't need a key or a coin to pry them out and end up breaking at least one nail in the process), you'll probably need to replace your outlet covers with the child-safe variety that automatically obscure the outlet when not in use. Before you start working with gadgets, however, see first how many outlets can be covered by simply moving heavy furniture in front of them. Anchor bookshelves and other pieces of furniture to the wall. If you have support beams or pillars in the room (common in many basements) surround them with shock absorbent padding to avoid a few trips to the emergency room. If there are any hazardous or potentially dangerous chemicals or detergents in or near the playroom, move them up and completely out of reach. If your playroom is in the basement, make sure that there is some form of outside access, be it a large window or door, in case of fire.

DEAL WITH THE WALLS: Mud, paint, apple juice, and coffee should all be able to bounce right off the surface, so choose a semigloss paint that's easy, easy, easy to clean. You also might want to take a pass on those fancy murals that you see in all the magazines. We promise, you and your kids will get sick of what's up there in a jiff. Better ideas? Our Girlfriend Tula simply started taping up all of her children's paintings and art projects. Over the years, her walls became an ever-changing chronicle of their creative development—and the cumulative effect was pretty fantastic. If you have any kind of artistic ability or inclination, paint an array of colorful "frames" directly on the wall and display your child's artwork by sticking it inside the "frames" with double-sided tape. Our Girlfriend Anne—who was a bit more protective of her playroom's paint job (it was a gorgeous, florid purple) strung clotheslines around the perimeter of the room and hung her kids' artwork with clothespins. (The lines were, of course, high enough off the ground not to entangle or choke anyone.) Other cool options you might consider for the walls: Paint a portion with chalkboard paint to create a built-in drawing surface (black isn't the only option anymore; Crayola offers a wide spectrum of bright colors). Or put up an expanse of corkboard to display artwork. Our Girlfriend Jessie, who's more evolved on the home-decorating front than many of us, went to a local school-supply store and bought an inexpensive alphabet chart and a couple of world maps. She threw them into a few simple frames from the hobby store and she had some cute decorations for her girls' playroom walls.

BUY A WORK/PLAY TABLE: Even if you have one of these in the kitchen, you'll need another for the playroom. If you must, buy a cute wooden set from a fancy catalogue; a molded plastic kid-size picnic table will do the trick, too. If you have space, it's not a bad idea to keep a larger table in the playroom with a couple of grown-up-size chairs as well. It'll come in handy for spreading out materials and you'll appreciate having somewhere to sit while you gobble down whatever meal you didn't have a chance to eat in the kitchen. You might also consider putting an easel in the playroom.

PUT TOGETHER A CRAFTS CABINET: Even with a mini arsenal in your kitchen, you should have an additional—and generally more elaborate—setup in your playroom. If you don't have built-in cabinets for the job, think about purchasing a multi-drawered cabinet on wheels from one of those container stores or catalogues. In addition to what we've listed in the kitchen arsenal (including another set of old T-shirts or smocks), you should stock this one with all sorts of odds and ends—fabric swatches, paper towel and toilet paper tubes, rubber bands, string. You never know what might come in handy for art projects. Keep a plastic tarp or shower curtain liner folded up inside or nearby the craft cabinet. It will come in very, very handy for all kinds of messy and not-so-messy endeavors.

SET UP SOME CLEANING SUPPLIES: Again, the easier it is to clean up, the more inclined you'll be to let your kids get creative. Stash a few rolls of paper towels, glass cleaner, and an all-purpose cleaner in a cabinet or shelf that's up out of reach. If possible, get a Dustbuster for the playroom, too. (Come to think of it, just about every floor of your home should have one.)

CREATE A COZY CORNER: Stick a couch you don't really care about in one area. If the floor is carpeted, you can even get away with just a few beanbag chairs or a bunch of oversize pillows. Add a soft, machine-washable fleece blanket because kids love to feel all safe and tucked in while in their cozy spots. Keep books and other reading materials handy in a nearby bookshelf or fill an oversize basket with current favorites and put it right on the floor. If you're putting a TV in the playroom, this is where it will go, as will a stereo or boom box. It's ideal if you can put all this electronic stuff in an armoire or cabinet that can be closed up. This way it can be kept out of sight—and out of harm's way—when you want it to be.

THINK STORAGE, STORAGE, STORAGE: Playroom cleanup should be an absolute no-brainer, for you and for your children. That means there should be plenty of space and plenty of containers, so no one has to go searching for an available spot to stow stuff. Keep toys basically organized—dress up in one box, wooden blocks in another, trucks on a particular shelf, musical instruments somewhere else. But don't go to extremes—if you insist that each of those elaborate Lego sets with the four million eensy teensy pieces be sorted separately and that every crayon goes right back in its sixty-four-piece box, you will resent cleaning up and your children may not even attempt it. If your child is a real stickler about keeping his favorite K'NEX or Lego sets together, you'll all be better off if he keeps those toys in his room. A good way to think about it: Your playroom should be organized in such a way that if a complete stranger were to come and clean up, it would be fairly obvious where everything should go. Start teaching the kids that their games will "die" instantly if they don't help with the cleanup.

Storage: A Place for Everything and Everything Somewhere Near It

Bookshelves: Low, wide bookshelves are great for storing videos, toys, and—yeah—books. Avoid storing toys behind one another—it's too tricky for kids to take things out and put them away on their own (which is the goal here). If you will be using freestanding bookshelves, be sure to anchor them against the wall.

Medium-size plastic storage bins: Use these for little stuff like Matchbox cars, action figures, Barbie accessories, etc. Go for clear ones when possible; avoid piling them one on top of the other and keep the covers off.

Toy trunk: If you happen to have one of these and it's designed with a child-safe lid that won't pinch fingers or trap anyone inside, keep it in the playroom but don't use it for toys. Trunks are too deep and it's far too tempting to use them as catchalls for homeless objects. Use your trunk instead for dress-up stuff or for large, chunky items like helmets and small sports accessories. (Note: Vicki has dealt with head lice infestations four times and just can't resist adding that helmets should never be shared, nor should hats, scarves, or hair decorations. It's just an unnecessary hassle. Stick to high heels, wings, capes, and Belle gowns and let the headdress be personal.)

Laundry baskets: We mentioned these before. They're inexpensive, colorful, very portable, and great for holding anything but items that are small enough to fall through the holes. Label them in general categories with a nice, fresh Sharpie (you may need to use a sticker). First, it's a mini-lesson in word recognition, which is pre-reading, no matter how you fry it, and second, kids are fond of categorizing. Let them choose the sorting system. It may be "All things that can fly," or "All dollies who aren't babies," or "All things to whack a new baby with when mom's not looking." Even if they're not up to reading, it helps the cleaner-upper with sorting at the end of the day.

Plastic toolboxes and tackle boxes: If you can find them (try craft stores), clear plastic ones are ideal. Use these for storing collections like beads, rubber stamps, etc. To avoid having tiny pieces strewn all over the playroom and a hysterical little collector, keep collection boxes with lots of little pieces in your child's room—if possible.

Wet wipes containers: These are great for holding all kinds of small stuff—stringing beads, rubber stamps, mini dinosaurs. Since most wet wipes containers are opaque, keep the top open so your kids can see what's in there. Our semi-compulsive Girlfriend Pam goes so far as to cut out or draw a picture of what's inside each and tape it to the box. Cute idea—but most of us can't be bothered. Vicki just attacks it with her trusty Sharpie.

Resealable plastic bags, small and large: Have a stash of these at the ready (and out of children's reach) in your playroom. Then, when the box for your son's favorite puzzle disintegrates (cut the picture of the puzzle out of the box cover and put it in the bag); when you want to grab a handful of Magic Markers for a long car ride at the last minute; when your daughter's playdate wants to bring home her still-wet craft creation, you will have just the right quickie, see-through container on hand.

GREAT BASICS FOR A PLAYROOM:
Soft foam blocks
Wooden unit blocks (once children are older and are less likely to klunk each other)
Exercise mats
Dress-up clothes and accessories (no hats or other head toppers—it's that head lice thing again).
Pretend housekeeping toys and accessories
Pretend tool bench
Toy trains and a table dedicated to their use alone, like the Thomas the Tank Engine set
Pop-up tent or cardboard playhouse
Lightweight balls

TIP: The Beauty of Butcher Paper

There's nothing like a huge expanse of paper to get a young imagination going. Lots of us have invested in a roll of kraft or butcher paper so we always have a fresh canvas on hand. On many occasions, we'll simply tape a big piece of it to the floor and let the kids go nuts. This thick, durable stock comes in approximately 800-foot-long rolls, in a variety of widths, ranging from about twelve to forty-eight inches. Kraft paper is traditionally (but not always) brown; butcher paper (which is actually used by butchers for wrapping meat) can come in brown, pink, or white. Both papers do a similar job. You can pick up kraft paper at an art supply store (they'll also sell you a piece if you don't want to buy a whole roll) or through a paper source like www.artstuff.net. Another good source with competitive prices and big variety: a food service supplier. Try Food Service Direct at www.foodservicedirect.com.

The Bedrooms

Most of the Girlfriends have found that our kids didn't really start hanging out on their own in their bedrooms (with their eyes open, at least) until they were old enough to realize mom and dad really weren't the coolest people on the planet. That highly misguided moment seems to occur sometime between the ages of seven and ten, depending upon your child's gender, temperament, and the layout of your home. In general, however, if you live in a house, your child's bedroom may actually see relatively little action during the early years. With that in mind, you probably won't need to buy or build tons of toy storage or make major accommodations for messy activities. It also means that if you're bent on doing something sort of darling for your child, his or her bedroom may indeed be the place to do it. (Again, think temporary. Accessorize, rather than build in. Her penchant for all things ballerina may, unfortunately, give way to an obsession with one of Britney Spears's belly button–baring successors at some point down the line.) And all the play stuff will eventually have to make way for a proper desk with a good lamp and storage space for a computer complete with CD burner, not to mention a place to charge her cell phone.

When you think about what type of fun stuff should go in a young child's bedroom, think about the sort of wind-down activities that happen around bedtime. You'll want bookshelves for books as well as favorite toys, and treasures. If stuffed animals are a major plague in the house, consider stringing up a toy hammock—it's literally a net that keeps stuffed toys up and off the floor. A play table or desk stocked with minimally messy materials like crayons, markers, and paper is always a great addition, if you have space. As for a TV in a child's bedroom—as you can pretty much guess, the Girlfriends aren't into the idea. If you are in the financial position to be considering a computer for your child's bedroom—put the computer in a shared family space instead so you can stay on top of what your little technowizard is up to and control how much time he's spending on the machine, at least till he has enough homework to warrant his own private laptop or whatever. Then, mom and dad, you will have to spy on him *in there* to make sure you haven't lost him to the vortex of crummy chats and worse graphics.

Your Home Office

If you work out of a home office, it's not a bad idea to keep a basket of toys, some crayons and paper, and a small table with chairs in your office. Not that you want your kids tromping up there every five seconds, but there will be times this stuff comes in handy. It'll buy you five minutes when you simply have to make a business call and there's no one else in the house on child duty. As your kids get a bit older, providing them with their own work space is a wonderful way to fit in some buddy time or homework time after school.

The Bathroom

A good, long, warm, bubbly bath can be one of the world's most relaxing experiences for a mom. And we're not even talking about you being in it. The simple fact that bathtime can delight, entertain, and even soothe a child and demands very limited movement on our part is enough to make it one of our very favorite playtime tactics. Harness bath toys in one of those net sacks that suctions to the tub. Keep a stash of plastic containers, even a small watering can on hand—whatever keeps your babe interested and laughing. As for your comfort—think about keeping a small chair or even a step stool in the room so you can give your knees and back a break. Girlfriends Kelly and Vicki sit on one of those big, blow-up exercise balls that gyms and labor wards are using these days. Vicki swears it's a great spine stretch and makes scooting around the tub a breeze, and she loves the bonus multitasking points.

The Yard

There are a bunch of things you can do to make your yard a more interesting and relaxing place for you and your young kids to spend time together. If it's at all possible, one of the best moves you can make is to fence or gate off some smallish section so you won't have to chase anyone too far when you don't want to. It'll also reduce your stress level, since you won't have to be as paranoid about little people slipping out of sight and running into traffic. Also, keep major attractions—like the sandbox—relatively close to the house. The kids will be more inclined to use them and it will be more convenient for you to keep them company. Another key is not to allow small toys or anything with lots of parts and pieces beyond, say, the patio or even better—out the door. Believe us—there is absolutely nothing more tedious than hauling everyone out into the yard every summer evening so you can round up countless pieces of plastic hidden in the grass. Except, perhaps, soothing your spouse after he steps on one of those things in his bare feet. So when you think of outside fun stuff, think big, easy to see, and easy to store. Here are some simple outside attractions that have given many of the Girlfriends a great run for the money:

THE KIDDIE PICNIC TABLE: Whether you pick up a cute wooden classic at a garden center or opt for a molded plastic version from your local superstore, you'll find these scaled-down tables with built-in seats indispensable. They're not just great for feeding the kids during the warm months—they're perfect for crafts projects. And as we cleaner-uppers all know, doing crafts outdoors beats doing crafts indoors any day of the week. Some of the Girlfriends actually use one kid-size picnic table as their children's play table year-round and move it in or out of doors, depending upon the season.

BIG PLASTIC STORAGE BIN: This should have a cover on it so it doesn't collect water. A drainage hole in the bottom is extra nice. Only allow big stuff—balls, plastic bats, etc., to be thrown in here. Otherwise you'll risk never seeing the small stuff again.

PLASTIC WAGON: Yeah, those classic wooden wagons are adorable, but after a few good rainstorms (which they are bound to be left out in), they peel and rust like crazy. Go with a big, chunky molded plastic version and you'll never have to think twice about it. They're great for toting stuff or little humans around the yard. They make cleanup a breeze and are good for storing smallish items, too. Just remember that even a quiet wagon ride requires the wearing of a helmet. These things start calmly and escalate into mayhem as soon as mom turns her back for one instant and allows the big four-year-old brother to pull his eighteen-month-old sister around the patio corners like a game of Crack the Whip.

VEGETABLE GARDEN: Even if you only have room for a few tomato plants, a garden can be hugely inspiring for you and your kids. Little people love getting dirty, using watering hoses, and seeing big, red, ripe veggies grow magically on the vine. You'll love having a project that has an actual payoff—like the smiles on your kids' faces when you come to the table with a plate full of what they've harvested. The National Gardening Association runs a terrific website, www.kidsgardening.com, that's brimming with information and age-appropriate ideas that will help get you started.

KIDDIE POOL: A small, inexpensive kiddie pool provides lots of wet fun without making the muddy mess that a sprinkler does. Since it's small and portable (you need to watch young children at all times when they are near it, anyway) you can put it right where it's convenient and comfortable for you to hang out. It does tend to kill the lawn underneath, so move it every day to let the sun do its healing. And, *please,* remember, an unsupervised baby or toddler can drown in an inch or two of water so never leave them alone, even in the baby pool.

SPRAY BOTTLES: There's something about these that makes them absolutely irresistible to kids of all ages. Buy a bunch of empty ones at the hardware store or warehouse club and keep them in the outdoor toy box. You will not believe how much the children will use them. For safety's sake, mark all bottles to be used by your kids "water only" since one of the most irresistible things to do with them, besides spraying mommy in the face with them, is to suck or spray the water into their own mouths. Keep this in mind whenever you make up your own cleaning solvents and use generic bottles—little kids won't know the difference and will spray and suck with abandon. Try making water bottles a different color entirely and lock up everything that's not good to drink.

THE SANDBOX: There are some lovely wooden ones out there, but they're expensive and can be a big pain to get rid of when the time finally comes. If you can bear it, think about one of those big, plastic, animal-shaped ones that comes with a cover. The cover is particularly fabulous if there are cats in your neighborhood because, in the middle of the night while they're carousing, they will turn your lovely sandbox into their private potty. Put it in a shady spot, and let the kids have fun. *House & Garden* won't want to shoot it, but who cares.

PLASTIC PLAYHOUSE: Kids love a cozy space—especially outside. Molded plastic playhouses may not be as gorgeous as some custom-made wooden beauties, but they require zero in the way of maintenance and really take plenty of punishment. (Vicki and her Girlfriend Sonia spent half a day putting one together while they were both pregnant, and they suggest you make your husband or the gardener or anyone else who's fairly strong and can read diagrams do it for you. If you must, bribe them with twenty-five dollars.) You also won't think twice about getting rid of the thing when your kids no longer use it: Our Girlfriend Jessie put hers out on the curb one Sunday afternoon and it had disappeared by suppertime. Vicki, however, still has her house and her castle because she is not emotionally ready for such things to disappear from her yard. She's considering therapy and her husband is threatening to toss them one day when she's busy being snack mom for soccer.

SWING SET: This is a toughie. Kids really do use their swing sets when they're young. The downside is swing sets—especially those big wooden doozies that are so popular now—are a big investment and are pretty much in your yard for good. We guess it all depends upon how many kids, how much extra space, and how many bucks you've got. One savvy strategy: See which of your neighbors have swing sets and encourage your kids to make friends with theirs. Vicki finally broke down and bought one of those redwood models after the birth of her third child and had to add an infant swing when baby number four came along. The kids used it nearly every single day of the year, if not to swing or slide, then just to sit on and talk and tell secrets. When they moved, they left the swing set behind and the kids have been in mourning for the four years since.

THE NETTED TRAMPOLINE: Vicki was terrified of trampolines because she had heard about so many wrist fractures and scraped legs, not to mention the possible head injuries associated with the most popular backyard plaything in the world. Then she found a decent, actually quite large, trampoline in the Hammacher Schlemmer catalog that was completely surrounded in netting up to about six feet. She has owned one for four years and, knock wood, no injuries. The only challenge is keeping more than one, or maybe two, kids off at a time. When the tramp is popping five or six kids left and right, it's a certain forehead bonking situation.

BALLS OF EVERY KIND: Think soccer balls, Nerf balls in all shapes because they don't hurt, basketballs, Wiffle balls, huge blow-up balls—anything that's fun to kick and throw around, weather-proof, and brightly colored so it's easy to find. Just be prepared; where balls go, bats follow and that takes a lot of supervision, not to mention helmets or other preventative measures. Even if you refuse to buy a bat, a stake will be pulled from your rosebushes or the cardboard inside of paper towels will be brought in as a surrogate. There's just something testosterone-driven about han-dling a ball and wanting to whack it hard.

The Rest of the House

In case you're rolling your eyes right now and muttering some-thing to the effect that "all that Girlfriendly advice is well and good if you want your kids running the entire house, but— Hey!—I want a pretty living room and my vision doesn't include large pieces of molded plastic," let us clarify here. The Girl-friends aren't saying that every corner of your house has to be child and toy infested. We've ticked off the main family hot spots where it will be easiest to spend time with your children. There are plenty of spaces, however, that can still be designated as off limits for general hijinks. We're talking living room, dining room, mom and dad's room, the library, the billiards room, the massage salon, the paddleball courts, the aviary (okay, we're just kidding on these last ones), etc. Heck, if you're really brave, go ahead and buy some nice stuff for these spots. (Though we still recommend against fine fabrics and carpets until the kids are at least past their grape juice and greasy fingers days.) Keep in mind, too, that if you're hell-bent on spending money, now may be the time to take on the structural stuff that's tough for kids to trash: Landscape your property, fix up the bathrooms, do the kitchen, build storage cabinets, pave the driveway, upgrade the gutters, finish the basement. You get the picture.

The Small Quarters Quotient

When our Girlfriend Lauren and her husband, Steve, were expecting for the first time, a cousin was nice enough to give them a hand-me-down high chair. The two toted the thing up to their tidy 900-square-foot apartment and were horrified to see how the light blue plastic clashed with the stylishly rustic oak-and-pine motif of their one common living area. (The kitchen wasn't an option since it was just big enough to accommodate a person and a blender at the same time.) Every time Lauren opened the door to her apartment during the months before she was due, her eyes landed on that light blue plastic and she would gag. She made a note that the chair would have to go and they would need to find something that blended in better. Flash forward to little Danny's second birthday. Lauren and Steve's apartment is unrecognizable. Circus-hued hulks of molded plastic consume practically every square inch of open space. Toy trucks of every shape and color line the perimeter of the room. Lauren helps Danny unwrap a gigantic present from his grandma: It's a plastic pretend kitchen that practically outsizes the real one. Lauren makes a mental note: "Get rid of oak side table next to couch. That wood clashes with all our plastic."

If you, like Lauren, live in tight quarters, the kid-stuff invasion is particularly intense. Storage is minimal and there's often no distinction between what serves as the living room, dining room, and family room. That's because, of course, it's all the same common space. Girlfriends in this situation who didn't want their one main room cluttered with junk have generally opted to use their child's bedroom as the place for toy storage and playdates. We simply accepted the fact that stuff would regularly come creeping out of there into the family space and got used to putting it away on a constant basis. (Which wasn't really such a big deal, since we didn't exactly have a long distance to drag it.) Eventually, most of us moved to a lower-rent district so we could ultimately live in a larger space with our children and avoid drowning in our own family clutter.

Hunt Down a Waterproof Blanket

When our Girlfriend Jamie gave birth to her second child several springtimes ago, she was eager to hang around outside with her brood. But the grass was still damp, the ground was sorta muddy, and Jamie knew she would need some kind of dry and comfortable surface on which she could plop her newborn—and her own hiney. Scouring the Internet, she came upon the absolute perfect thing: a fleecy dark blue hunting blanket that had a rubbery waterproof coating on one side. (The "waterproof" coating was actually intended to protect a hunter's car from whatever gory thing he was dragging home.) Well, Jamie loved her waterproof hunting blanket for far more peaceful pursuits and it became her baby present of choice for many of us. We Girlfriends used Jamie's waterproof gift blankets not only for playing and picnicking outside on the lawn, on the deck, or on family vacations, but as cozy drop cloths indoors. Kids can spill, make a mess, eat, you name it, then the whole thing just gets popped into the washer and dryer. Over the years, the idea has obviously caught on. Lots of companies now make fancier versions—grown-up outlets like Orvis often sell theirs as "waterproof picnic blankets." Camping stores and catalogues like REI market them as waterproof outdoor blankets. The baby catalogues sometimes call them "waterproof play blankets." Some come in cute, colorful patterns. Many come with handy carrying straps. We tend to like the basic, no frills version so we don't have to worry about wear and tear or stains. Buy whatever suits you (as long as it can be machine washed and dried)—you'll find it indispensable . . . for years and years.

CHAPTER TWO

The Realist's Approach to Home Play

There are oodles of books, websites, and magazine articles filled with ultra-creative ideas about how to have fun with your kids. We think it's a great idea to check them out when you have the time, energy, and inclination. The Girlfriends are more interested, however, in providing you with some very basic concepts that can go the distance over time and that require minimal anxiety and effort on your part. Here's what's worked for us on the fun-making homefront:

Eight Enjoyable At-Home Activities (When You Have Some Active Brain Cells and a Bit of Energy)

1. **Hit the kitchen.** In general, we agree with the other parenting guides that cooking is a great activity to do with the kids.

But rather than devote an afternoon or evening to making silly children's recipes that you find in magazines, just invite your child to help you make real food that people are actually going to eat—have him clean and tear the lettuce for the salad; let him practice pounding the chicken cutlets with the tenderizing hammer; have them crack the eggs for cookies, serve some for dessert, and freeze what's left over. You never know, after years of preparing pasta primavera or your mother's famous apple cake, your kids may never even ask to make gelatin pizza or green pasta pancakes.

2. **Wash the car.** You may very well have to get the whole thing redone at the commercial car wash on the highway, but go ahead and descend upon your family jalopy with a hose, sudsy water, sponges, and rags. While the kids soak everything in sight and polish the hubcaps, you can crawl inside and pick out old Cheerios and Happy Meal remnants from under the car seats.

3. **Work in the garden or flower beds.** Show the kids the difference between nice plants and weeds. Let them go to town pulling up the latter. Just know that if you move on to another task, the weed pulling will come to a halt. Kids really do have this amazing ability to smell when play is just disguised work. A good strategy might be to give your little weed puller a small beach bucket and offer her an extra bedtime story or fifty cents if she fills it with weeds. It's never to early to teach a free market economy to the kids.

4. **Make a movie.** Brush the dust off the camcorder that hasn't been used since the last big birthday (or birth). Put on some cool tunes and shoot footage of the kids dancing around. Follow them with the camera as they give a tour

of their room or the whole house. Ask them to introduce each of their favorite dolls or stuffed animals on camera. Have them show off newly acquired skills—shoelace tying, pouring their own juice, setting the table. Sit down together and watch the flick when it's finished. And hold on to that tape. The everyday stuff is often far more amusing than the fancy occasions that are most often caught on camera. Then, if you're really ambitious or computer savvy, quickly transfer the videos to DVD. You'd be astonished to see how much color and definition gets lost on videotape over five to ten years. By the time you're trying to put a video montage together for a Bar Mitzvah or a Sweet Sixteen, you might be left with several shades of gray of your darling child's entire childhood. To us moms, this is a crisis as urgent as Hollywood rushing to restore all their old movies before the film disintegrates, so ask around if you need help. Anybody who can burn a CD can probably figure out how to make this transfer for you.

5. **Play beauty parlor.** Take out your old cosmetics, hair scrunchies, and nail polish. Let your daughter (yes, we're making an assumption here) do a number on you. This may even come a tiny bit close to mommy pampering. If the cleanup sounds too daunting, just pull out your favorite hand lotion and teach your child to give a hand massage. They're usually strong enough to be effective, plus you get to enjoy holding hands for the duration.

6. **Tackle a new board game.** Take advantage of your relatively sane state of mind and higher patience level. Pull out one of those games that have been sitting in shrink wrap since they arrived at the last birthday blitz. Learn how to play it along with your little one. Remember our smorgasbord theory;

there are some mothers who have absolutely refused to play all board games from Candy Land to Scrabble and their kids seem none the worse for the deprivation. Vicki, for one, gets all itchy when asked to play cards or board games, and we think she was entitled to draw the line at the unbearable. Take it from us, being a generous and giving mother does not require martyrdom. Life's too short.

7. **Get crafty.** Break out one of those boxed crafts kits that's left over from the last birthday haul. Or tackle any of the simple suggestions we've listed in our craft section.

8. **Put together an indoor picnic.** Who cares what it's doing out? Decorate paper plates with the kids, make peanut-butter-and-banana sandwiches, rustle up some good cookies for dessert, then head off with your basket to some cozy corner of the house. Hang out on an old blanket in your shorts, eat lunch, then read and do some bead stringing. To make it even more authentic, drape a blanket over the coffee table or across the sofa and make a tent. Kids love the close quarters.

How to Play Without Moving Your Body (Too Much)

For those occasions when you're so mentally and physically pooped that simply breathing is a feat in itself—try one of these slacker activities on for size:

1. **Get out old photos.** Snuggle up somewhere comfy with your little one and go through favorite family vacation and holiday photos. Baby and wedding albums are also a

big hit. If you can muster the energy to tell the two most precious tales in your child's universe, The Day You Were Born and/or How Daddy and Mommy Fell in Love and Married, you'll become a superhero. If you've told the story before (and we're sure you have), you might get away with just beginning each part of the tale and letting your kiddo finish it for you.

2. **Sort coins.** Empty out the family change bucket or piggy bank, separate coins into piles, and put them into sleeves (most banks give them out for free). Remind the little ones (and yourself) how filthy those coins can be so wash up well before snacking, picking your nose, or putting your fingers in your little brother's eye.

3. **Organize and categorize your child's bookshelf with her help.** Guaranteed—you will wind up discovering—and reading—old and new favorites. Get as sidetracked as time allows; this is not really about installing the Dewey decimal system. If you don't finish the job, just stack up the mess you've made and wait for another rainy day. Along the same lines, don't limit story time to bedtime. Pull out books whenever it strikes you and read in all kinds of fun spots—by a cozy fire in the living room, out on the hammock, on the front stoop.

4. **Go online.** Do random searches for favorite sports figures, weird bugs, ballerinas, etc. Print out cool pictures you find. Keep a collection in a spare photo album or ring binder if you want. Kids love to collect clip art to send to friends, to print and color, or even to cut out and make collages. You can even suggest they trace or try to draw freehand the picture they've discovered.

5. **Sit outside and blow soap bubbles.** Let your child or children chase them. Help them keep a tally. Challenge them to see who can blow more on one breath or how many "twin," "triplet," or "quadruplet" bubbles they can attach to each other. If you have a dog who is kid-safe, see if he likes to eat bubbles—it can be hysterical for little kids to watch that commotion.

6. **Play doctor and you be the very, very, very ill or injured patient** (of course, don't contract anything too scary sounding. Think Bent Backward Fingers or Broken Head or Leg Not Working, or something else along those lines). Let the kids minister to you while you lie nearly comatose. Have your child wrap your "wounds" with dish towels or, for real authenticity, keep a couple of Ace bandages on hand for this game. Our Girlfriend Lorraine has actually made an "emergency kit" with a play thermometer, a tin of Band Aids from Costco, and an Ace bandage.

7. **Play cards.** (Unless it makes you anxious and itchy, like Vicki). Teach your child how to play extremely simple card games that require no concentration whatsoever on your part. War is a good one—our Girlfriend Stacy swears she can actually sleep while she plays this game with her son. The website www.pagat.com provides rules and information about every card game you can possibly think up. Isn't it just brilliant what the Internet can provide? If you're not a card shark, puzzles are another excellent stay-in-one-spot option. Our Girlfriend Rhea really has catnapped unnoticed through many fifty-piece or more jigsaw puzzles.

8. **Play gas station.** Sit down at the end of your driveway and pretend that you're the gas station attendant. If it's summer, lie in a child's blue plastic pool for heat relief. Who cares what the neighbors say? Have your child ride up on his trike or bike. You fill him up with gas and give him a travel advisory ("Looks like there's a fender bender on Route Nine," "The toll guy says you have to sing all the way to Boston," etc.). Let him ride down the driveway and back, while you sip a cool drink. Kind of makes you wish you lived on a country estate with a five-mile road leading to the house, doesn't it?

9. **Pull out the tape recorder.** Moving your voice box isn't nearly as tiring as moving your body. Kids are also absolutely enthralled with the whole idea of hearing themselves on tape. Sing songs. Make pig sounds. Tell stories. Record a "letter" to Grandma and send it off in the mail. You get the idea.

10. **Bead it.** Talk about a fabulously mesmerizing activity. Keep a tackle or toolbox full of different colored beads and string at the ready. Pull it out when you're pooped, sit down somewhere comfortable, and make cool necklaces, bracelets, etc., with your sidekick. If you don't have beads, Cheerios, Froot Loops, and uncooked tubular pasta work well, too. Obviously, keep small beads out of reach of kids who are liable to eat them or stick them up their nose and don't, under any circumstance, allow younguns to get at the beads if you won't be on hand supervising—you'll still be finding the things under the beds, in the couch and in the carpet weave when you send your last child off to college.

11. **Play hide-and-seek.** Our Girlfriend Kelly grabs a copy of *InStyle* and hides very, very well.

Easy Projects for the Artistically Challenged

For those of us who don't have any particular talent in the art department, sitting down to draw or color with the kids is like sitting down at the piano when you can't read music. It's fun to mess around for a while. But what then? How do you keep things interesting?

That's probably why there are all those websites and books brimming with nifty ideas for arts and crafts projects. A project adds some much welcomed structure to creativity. Kids get to learn a little about something new. You both have a goal to work toward. And they walk away with something cool they've made themselves.

The problem for the Girlfriends is that sometimes all those ultra-creative arts and crafts projects are just too darned complicated. The directions can be so rigid that trying to follow them becomes a trial in itself. And all of those materials? A magazine editor or a kindergarten teacher might have stuff like foam core and florists wire on hand all the time, but we sure don't. As we see it, if a spur-of-the-moment project requires a pilgrimage to the crafts store, a Valium, or an engineering degree, it sort of defeats the whole purpose. Here are simple ways we've found to have some ongoing, artsy fun without too much in the way of parental talent or exotic materials.

GREAT ARTIST INSPIRATIONS. Go online and look up a favorite painter (abstract masters like Mark Rothko and Jackson Pollock are particularly great for younger kids, as well as for those of us who don't have a prayer of drawing anything that looks like anyone or any particular object). Pick a few paintings with your child and print them out. Using these as inspiration, paint or color your own works of art.

COMPLETELY COLORED PAPER. Pull out a nice, big, spankin' fresh piece of newsprint or drawing paper and a basket full of crayons. Sit down at the kitchen or play table with your child and aim to scribble on every single smidgen of empty space on the paper. Use every different color crayon you have. Believe it or not, this (a) takes up a nice chunk of time, (b) is brainless yet sort of fun to accomplish, (c) provides a relaxed vibe that encourages conversation to flow, and (d) produces a piece of art that's pretty darned terrific-looking. You can take all of this a step further by coloring over the whole masterpiece with black crayon (this isn't such a daunting task if you use a smallish piece of paper). Then scratch through the black crayon with a popsicle stick to let the colors show through.

SPONGE PAINTING. Cut kitchen sponges into random shapes. Pour some tempera paints into shallow bowls or the lids of plastic containers. Dip sponges in and decorate large pieces of paper. Use the finished masterpiece as gift wrap.

ROCK PAINTING. Go out to the yard and find some interesting rocks. Craggy, bumpy ones, smooth river stones, they're all good. In terms of size, fist-sized rocks are about right since they provide just enough surface space and can be used as paperweights (what else does a kid give dad on Father's Day?). After washing and drying them, decorate them using plain old washable paints and brushes on a newspaper-covered table. This is a great activity for siblings of different ages since the older children can work with the rock's natural contours and textures to create something specific, like a bumpy toad or a ladybug. (Older kids can use acrylic paints for a more polished and permanent result.)

FAVORITE THINGS COLLAGE. Keep a stack of old magazines and catalogues in your crafts closet, especially those with kid-friendly themes like seed and gardening catalogues, food magazines, toy catalogues, and sports weeklies. Whenever the opportunity arises, drum up a themed collage idea with your child—it could be all pink, all flowers, cool sports stars, favorite foods, or things that start with a "b." Use glue sticks to affix your finds onto a piece of construction paper. Covering the finished masterpiece on both sides with clear contact paper gives you a cool place mat.

THE BEST HOMEMADE PLAY-DOH. Every crafts website and activities book in the universe offers their recipe for this soft, moldable dough. The Girlfriends have tried a whole bunch of versions and think this formula is perfection. It's nice and pliant, stays moist, doesn't stick, and is really easy to make. Make it once and you may never go back to using the crumbly store-bought stuff. Here's how:

1. Have the kids help you dump the following ingredients into a heavy 6-quart saucepan: 2 cups flour, 1 cup salt, 4 teaspoons cream of tartar, 2 cups water, and 4 tablespoons vegetable oil.

2. Cook on very low heat, stirring constantly with a wooden spoon until the mixture thickens, pulls away from the sides of the pot, and begins to form a ball.

3. Empty dough onto a clean work surface and knead until smooth. Divide dough according to the number of colors you want to make. Pat each ball flat, add several drops of the food coloring of choice (sugar-free Kool-Aid also works and makes the dough smell great), and knead it in until the color is uniform. Add more color, depending on how bright you want the dough to be. Stored in separate resealable plastic bags, this dough will keep for many weeks. When it gets dirty or stiff, simply toss it and make a new batch.

CARDBOARD CUTOUTS. Don't send all of your cardboard trash to be recycled—recycle some of it yourself by using it as a nice, stiff canvas for all kinds of projects. Pick out some big flat pieces with your child and talk about what might be fun to make. Use a pencil or pen to sketch out a simple, rudimentary shape—no one's watching here, so just have fun. Draw the outline of an umbrella, a doll, or two high heeled shoes. Sketch the basic shape of a rocket or if it's not too politically incorrect in your book, a (blunt) sword and shield. Using a big pair of scissors or a box cutter (and keeping your child out of harm's way), cut along the lines. Then have a blast decorating the cutouts with your child. Crayons, paint, glitter sticks, stickers—it's all good stuff. And since these pieces are pretty sturdy, they'll get plenty of mileage on the pretend front after they're finished.

CREATE YOUR OWN "STAINED GLASS" WINDOWS. This is a variation on the nature prints idea that Vicki recalled from her vague and distant childhood and shared with her own kids. For once, her idea was a success! She and her kids found autumn leaves or flower petals and placed them on a square (about twelve inches) of waxed paper. For extra pizzazz they added shavings from crayons, confetti, or any other flat, small bits of stuff. Then they put another piece of waxed paper on top of the array and Vicki slipped it onto a towel so that she could bond the creation with the household iron on a low setting. Then the wax "windows" were hung up in all sun-exposed windows for maximum effect. The crayon shavings really were the most fabulous part, so if you want to skip the nature part because it's snowing or your allergies are acting up, feel free to ad lib on this theme. One last tip: If you get crayon wax on your iron, just turn it on high and run it over a couple of paper towels. That should avoid it getting on the collar of your husband's favorite Hawaiian shirt.

MARBLE PAINT. Get your hands on a cardboard box top that has low sides—a shirt box is good. Place a piece of construction paper in the box to cover the bottom. Squirt or dab some tempera paints onto the paper and toss in a marble or two. Let your kids tilt the box around so the paint-covered marble creates a cool abstract design.

MAKE PASTA ART. Before you breathe one word about this project to the kids, boil up a batch of spaghetti until they are soft but not mushy (add a touch of oil to the water before you add the noodles so they won't stick together). Drain the spaghetti in a colander, then run cold water over the noodles until they are cool to touch. Then call in the kids and plop the pasta in the middle of a table. Give the kids a piece of dark construction paper to decorate (black is very nice) and let them "draw" with the noodles by pressing them onto the paper. They can use butter knives to cut the noodles into shorter lengths or simply pinch them into pieces. The natural starch in the noodles will keep the "drawing" in place once they dry, but only for a day or two so conveniently "lose" the starchy creations or reglue them with Elmer's before you go to bed.

BASIC CRAFTY CREATIONS. Pull out those pipe cleaners and popsicle sticks (known sans ice cream as "craft sticks") and let your child build what she wants. She can twist the pipe cleaners around a pencil, pull them off and use the coil as a base for making crazy bugs. With the help of white glue, popsicle sticks can be used to spell out names and make shapes on construction paper or to build mini log cabins and other architectural showpieces.

Smart Ways to Keep a Kid Busy (While You Get Something Done)

LET HIM CLEAN THE KITCHEN. Children's love of spray bottles is almost as universal as their love of french fries. Why else do you think every kid under the age of about ten begs to help mom spritz the kitchen appliances and wash the windows? For a safer (and cheaper) alternative to massive Windex exposure, fill a spray bottle full of water. Give your helper some paper towels and let him clean, let him clean. You may have to do a little wiping to get rid of streaks when he's through—but hey, it's worth it.

LET 'EM POUR. Set a waterproof blanket on the kitchen floor (all you Californians, Arizonians, Floridians, and Hawaiians just walk outside). Pull out some different size plastic containers. Fill one with some water. Let toddlers practice pouring the water from one container to another. To make the game last longer, add some larger measuring spoons and slotted ladles. If you have a minute (and a child that's older than about four), show her how big a teaspoon is and ask her for three or four teaspoons of water in a glass. You could even go so far as to share the deep, dark cooking secret that a big T in a recipe means tablespoon and a little t means teaspoon. Apparently they're not teaching that in school anymore.

SET UP A SCAVENGER HUNT. Write out a list or draw pictures of common, easily and safely accessible objects around the house or yard. You might include a hairbrush, a spoon, a ball, a small toy car, a leaf, a crayon, a plastic container, a shoe, a beanbag toy, a Lego block, etc. Give your hunter a cool collection container—a fancy shopping bag or sand bucket is great. Then send your child out on his search while you do what you need to do. After each discovery, have him report what he's found so you can provide some encouragement. When he's found all the stuff—reward him with a big hug or some one-on-one play or snack time. If you still have more time to play (or just endure), help the kids create a list for you and have them send you off searching for stuff. If you're as lucky as most of us, they'll forget where you went for up to half an hour and you can have smelled all the perfume samples in *Allure* by then.

WASH THE TOYS. On a warm day (and when you can stay very close at hand), fill a bucket or pot with warm soapy water, fill up those spray bottles, and pull out a bunch of rags. Haul out all those yard toys—buckets, bats, ride ons, wagons, buggies—and let your kids give them a good wash. Little kids can be plunked right in front of a pan of water and charged with washing the smaller items. Bigger sibs can take on the larger stuff with their spray bottles. As always, exercise extreme caution when you are using water—young children can drown in a bucket, even if it's filled just a few inches.

RECONSIDER THE COMPUTER. CD-ROMs and the Internet aren't a child's only computer option. If you have a beginning reader, why not simply open a document for her and entertain all the possibilities a blank sheet has to offer? Sit down beforehand and write or help her write out a list of things in a particular category—ingredients for an imaginary meal, favorite animals, sports teams, every word she can think of that starts with T, names of relatives and friends, her list for Santa (that's an ace in the hole), etc. Then set her and her list up at the keyboard and let her type it all out. The novelty of it will undoubtedly enchant her. Once you teach the basics—how to use the space bar, how to hit the return—she can take off all on her own. Have her create and name a new document each time. Give her her own file.

As she gets more comfortable at the keyboard, teach her how to play with various fonts and type colors. With any luck, she might just be willing to take a new business proposal or quarterly earnings report off your plate.

PULL OUT A STICKER BOOK. Keep a bunch of these on hand but out of sight so it ups the fabulous factor when you take one out. Sit your child down at a table and let him go to town transferring the stickers to some other surface. As long he is dexterous enough to peel the stickers away from their backing (age three is about right), he won't need much input from you to stay entertained. Little kids can have fun simply filling a pad of paper with the stickers. Older kids can decorate a shoe box or even plastic drinking cups, which they can then set the table with for dinner.

Clever Ways to Make Pretend Play Less Painful

Give any kid between the ages of two and six the choice of what they want to do with mommy or daddy and chances are good they'll say the "P" word. You know what we're talking about: They want to pretend. This pursuit usually involves us grown-ups trying to follow some very kooky plot and our child telling us that whatever we are doing is wrong. Our minds become numb as we spray our six millionth invisible fire and our mommy bodies ache from crawling around and putting ourselves in unbelievably uncomfortable positions. Of all play, the Girlfriends have to say, pretend is the hardest. And wouldn't luck have it that experts say it's one of the most beneficial ways to interact with your child? Sometimes we Girlfriends feel that the experts are being passive-aggressive with us and we resent it. Nonetheless, here are our tips to make the proposition more enjoyable for everyone.

SET A TIME LIMIT. You will be far more inclined to put some energy into your act if you know that the pretend tea party isn't going to last all afternoon. Fifteen minutes is the max for most of us moms and seems to be plenty for our young pretenders. Set a kitchen timer to enforce the limit—that way your kid can be angry with the vague concept of the time-space continuum and leave us moms out of it.

KEEP YOUR EYE ON THE PRIZE. The point of playing tea party isn't so you can learn to distinguish oolong from Earl Grey. It's not really about playing tea party at all. It's about what naturally unfolds while you're playing. Step back a little and think about what your child is doing and saying—you'll probably learn a whole lot about what he's feeling and thinking in general, how his amazing little mind ticks, and which commercials are getting the most play on Nickelodeon and the Cartoon Network.

ASK QUESTIONS. Instead of simply trying to follow some mysterious plotline (and being in a complete and utter fog), go ahead and ask some offbeat, open-ended questions. Where did Mrs. Biggles buy her biscuits? How many kids does she have? What's her favorite snack? How do you know Mrs. Biggles? The answers can be intriguing and sometimes downright hysterical. This kind of verbal interaction—and general distraction—can also minimize how much you have to jump around and contort your body.

ADD A NEW TWIST. When our Girlfriend Brett plays tea party, she cuts out pictures of food with Suzanna and puts it on the plates. It adds a nice change from the same plastic piece of cake and rubber carrot that's always part of the party. They can then also focus on something specific—what they're eating, what letter the foods start with, if they are fruits or vegetables, etc.

MULTITASK WHILE YOU PRETEND. Our Girlfriend Haley has five kids and really can't stop everything to play. So she ties in her son Alden's pretend play with her to-do list. For example, Alden likes to pretend he's different exotic animals. So Haley pretends she's a zookeeper or pet shop owner and invites Alden the Animal to crawl after her as she gives him a tour of the house (and puts laundry away at the same time).

WEAR COMFORTABLE CLOTHING. Sitting or crawling around on the floor, which is where pretend play usually happens, is a lot less painful if your pants or some other article of clothing aren't cutting off your circulation. Your child has comfortable play clothes. So should you. If your kids begin vying for your attention the minute you come home from work, you should teach them that they will have much more fun with mommy if she has a chance to take her panty hose off and put on her sweats first.

TEACH SOMETHING REAL WHILE YOU'RE PRETENDING. If you're playing tea party, share your favorite banana bread recipe with your child, help her write it down, talk about how you make it. It's often easier to deal with the real than to purely pretend.

MAKE YOUR HUSBAND DO IT. Or your mom, for that matter. Need we elaborate?

The Essential Toys

A fun house has fun things to play with. Many of those things are toys (others are too precious or scary to mention). Here's an age-by-age list of the toys that have gotten the very most mileage in the Girlfriends' homes over the years. We know it will never satisfy you or the grandparents, so for more toy info, see page 223 in the party section.

AGES 1–2
Push toys
Soft, lightweight balls
Pounding bench
Cardboard blocks
Chunky plastic cars and
    trucks
Stacking toys
Shape sorters
Pop-up tent
Soft clutch dolls
Child-size tape recorder
Child-size carrying cases
    (toolboxes, purses,
    satchels)
Duplo Primo

AGES 2–3
Pretend food
Doll stroller
Magna Doodle
Wooden unit blocks
Large-piece wooden puzzles
Ride-on toys
Dollhouse
Pretend kitchen and other
    pretend housekeeping toys
    and accessories

Pretend tool bench
Child-size pretend phone
Sprinkler
Miniature play sets
    (such as Fisher-Price
    Little People)
Tricycle

AGES 3–4
Child-size musical instru-
    ments
Dress-up clothes
Doctor kit
Pretend furniture and acces-
    sories
Floor puzzles
Matchbox cars
Elaborate trucks
Easel
Wooden train set
Dress-up dolls
Real baby dolls
Basic Lincoln Logs
Giant Tinkertoys

AGES 4–5
Kid-size sport balls

Kid-size sports equipment, e.g., a T-ball stand, basketball net, soccer net
Simple board games
Pretend cash register
Felt board and felt sets
Positive, nonviolent action figures and dolls; animal figures; etc.
Playmobil
Child-size music keyboard
Bike with training wheels and helmet

AGES 5–6
Playing cards
Checkers and chess
Board games

Marbles
Jump rope
Child-size binoculars and other nature gear
Legos
Playmobil
Coloring books

AGES 6–7
Child-size gardening set
K'NEX and other construction sets
Jacks
Pick-up sticks
Child-sized Foosball table
Mancala
Board games

Educational, Shmeducational

The Girlfriends just have to laugh at the whole "educational toys" craze. We're not talking about the basics that have been around since we were kids, like blocks and shape sorters. We're talking about the high-tech contraptions that are touted to actually teach kids stuff all on their own: the expensive electronic busy boxes and books that claim to provide reading and math instruction; the computerized musical blocks that supposedly turn your child into a mini Mozart; the dolls designed to teach your child five different languages.

Well, we've got about a zillion of these things piled up in our basements and attics. And we can tell you that all they've taught our children and us is the difference between a AA, a C, and a D battery.

Almost to a one, our kids got these toys, fiddled with the buttons for a few days, and quickly lost interest. Sure, we could get our little ones to focus on a computerized phonics board for five minutes if we sat down with them. But simple letter blocks or books did the job just as nicely without all the annoying beeps and harsh-sounding electronic zombie voices.

Our point is that, in the Girlfriends' opinion, this heavy-handed high-tech take on "educational toys" is bunk. There's no reason to turn every aspect of young kids' lives into a force-fed ABC session and they're not going to buy into it anyway. The toys our children loved most were simple and open-ended. They allowed them to be creative and just plain have fun. As far as the Girlfriends are concerned—our kids learned a whole lot more from doing that than by sitting around with any droning piece of pedantic plastic that's out there.

CHAPTER THREE

Getting Out

After slogging our way through countless wide-open days when nothing special is planned (or when social engagements were cancelled due to someone's ear infection somewhere), the Girlfriends have all pretty much arrived at the same conclusion: The most exhausting way to spend this time is to stay put, no matter how fun your house is. That applies whether you're pacing around with a colicky baby, playing endlessly with your toddler or preschooler, or trying to keep siblings from killing each other. In other words, no matter how difficult or counterintuitive it may be to pack up and head out with baby or babies in tow, doing something for at least part of the day will ultimately be a more sanity-preserving, relaxing endeavor than staying in all day. This is largely because the simple change of scene is a form of entertainment itself—which gives you—the perpetual amusement provider—some much needed relief.

Where's a parent with young children to go and how do you do it? First, some basic advice:

KEEP IT SIMPLE. As you probably already know, when you're tooling around with young kids, everything takes a whole lot longer and everyone gets tired a whole lot faster. A bus ride to a children's museum and lunch to follow may seem like a fun-packed day but in actuality, any one of those activities—including the bus ride alone—is just about enough to provide the right dose of amusement. While you may want to hit three big box stores on the highway and get all the errands done at once, visiting more than one may transform the adventure from a hoot to a horror. You're much better off scaling back, tackling one store, and stopping for a cup of hot chocolate and coffee on the way home, if everyone's game. Believe it or not, even a simple escapade like that—and the potentially relaxing car time that goes with it—can make for a great afternoon.

BE PREPARED. Keep a bag in your car with emergency basics (extra diapers, wipes, bottles of water, Tylenol, cloth diapers, receiving blankets) as well as a full change of clothes so an exploding diaper or minor boo-boo won't send you scurrying to a drugstore or back to home plate. To avoid driving around in a frenzy searching out the nearest Happy Meal, bring basic snacks and drinks that will take the edge off little appetites. Always have an entertainment stash on hand—keep a ball in the bottom of every stroller; crayons, markers, and paper in your bag. At any given time, a person can find at least a couple of Matchbox cars in our Girlfriend Kate's coat pockets and handbags. Many of us have ended up borrowing them in a pinch.

OPT FOR SPOTS WITH ROOM TO ROAM. Instead of that quiet coffee shop with the booths where your baby napped so peacefully when she was a newborn, find a place for coffee that can accommodate a toddler's or preschooler's more active spirit. Starbucks, with its casual seating and open floor space, is a great example. Just keep the little ones away from the fruit juice case and holiday gift displays. Another good choice: pizzerias, and the café at your local Barnes & Noble. Our Girlfriend Stacy found safe harbor with her preschool son and daughter at her local indoor hockey rink. The upstairs observation level was a large, wide-open room without much that could be destroyed; watching the figure and hockey skaters in action down below provided some diversion for everyone. Popcorn and drinks for sale downstairs were an added bonus.

CONSIDER YOUR LITTLE DARLING'S INTERESTS. Once they're past babyhood, kids really do have interests of their own (even if those interests are as basic as "big furry things" or "stuff I can touch"). When those interests aren't satisfied, the crying and whining starts. So while an art museum might be a fine place to stroll around with an infant, you're much better off taking a toddler or preschooler to a natural history museum. It has those all-important open spaces plus big stuffed bears and moon rocks that will no doubt captivate your child's attention. (Just avoid things that might end up terrifying him or her. Our Girlfriend Felicia's toddler daughter cried so hysterically when she caught sight of a giant stuffed bear, she gagged and vomited a cheese dog all over Felicia in the middle of New York's Museum of Natural History.)

THINK OUT OF THE BOX. Children's museums. Puppet shows. Movie matinees. Play zones. Theme parks. On occasion, all of these classic family magnets can be a kick. Too much of this stuff, though, and the crowds and expense can make any parent positively percolate. Especially after we pay thirty dollars in admission, and junior takes five steps inside and decides he wants out.

Harking back to the whole concept of keeping things simple, consider outings that aren't so obvious or ambitious. There are plenty of places that really do seem utterly fascinating to young children, yet don't require earplugs, and in most cases, don't charge admission. The following spots are great for short outings on the weekend or just about any time you need an easy and amusing change of scene:

BREAKFAST: It'll get you up, dressed, and out of the house and set the day in motion. During the week, pop into Dunkin' Donuts for coffee and muffins. On the weekends, why not sit down at a diner and order up a real meal—it's an easy place to break young ones in to eating-out etiquette. It may also be the closest thing you and dad come to eating out for a while. You'll be amazed at how things might naturally unfold from there—you might stop at the barbershop next store and watch other little kids get their hair cut. Dad might be able to pick up some razors at the drugstore. You could buy a winning lottery ticket. Hey. You never know.

THE HOME DEPOT: Our Girlfriend Amanda and her husband regularly take their two young boys to Hardware Heaven on winter Saturdays and the guys couldn't be more enthralled if they were hanging out with Bob the Builder himself. At peak shopping times, all sorts of demonstrations are happening: Burly types are cutting tile, staining cabinets, drilling holes, you name it. Even if there's nothing special scheduled, kids can watch giant pieces of wood being sawed, explore mock kitchens in the home decorating department, and admire oodles of toilet seats displayed on the wall like priceless Rembrandts. Chances are good you can pick up something the house is sorely in need of (think lightbulbs, new air conditioner filters) or discover cool stuff for the kids (spray bottles, plastic tarps, foam paintbrushes, empty toolboxes, to name a few). *Important safety note: Warehouse stores aren't playgrounds and those heavy boxes and raw supplies can cause injuries if they fall or are mishandled. Keep a careful eye on your children at all times.*

PET STORE: To young kids, a shop filled with puppies, kittens, birds, and fish is as good as a zoo. If owning a pet is about as high on your list as buying a monster truck, play down the purchasing aspect of these spots. Should the issue come up, explain what allergies are and think of some relative or frequent visitor (even the mailman will do) whose condition prohibits you from bringing home a furry friend. At least for now.

BOOKSTORES AND YOUR LOCAL LIBRARY: By all means take advantage of the story hours and activities that many bookstores and libraries schedule these days. Also head over when nothing's going on—sitting down to read some new storybooks or simply letting your little one run around in the kids' section while you settle down on the floor with a pile of cookbooks is entertaining and relaxing all on its own. You might even meet some other moms and babes. If the place has a café, you're really in business. Many local libraries feature holiday events, craft sessions, computer classes, and reading clubs for kids, endless selections of magazines, videos, CD-ROMs, and every book in your kids' favorite series. It's never too early to teach them what a valuable asset your library is.

LOCAL SPORTS EVENTS: Parents of older kids are all too aware of the sports scene in town. For those of us in the new parenting bubble, however, local games often don't even appear on our radar. That's a missed opportunity. To young kids, a high school soccer, baseball, field hockey, ice hockey, or lacrosse game (heck, even a practice) can be almost as impressive as a major league event. They can watch as much or as little as they want—there's often no admission and you can come and go as you like. For us mommies, it's a chance to hang out around other big humans and let the kids roam the sidelines (while we keep an eye on them, of course). Our Girlfriend Maryann, whose husband works late, packs up a picnic about once a week during the spring and eats dinner with her toddler and kindergartner while watching their Saturday night sitter play on their local high school softball team. For a big night out, take the kids to a minor league baseball game, if you have a team in your area. It's friendly, the field is nice and close in, and the cost is a fraction of what you'll pay at a major stadium.

BALLET OR KARATE/TAE KWON DO STUDIOS: Along the same lines as the above suggestion, pop in on one of these local studios and check out what the kids are up to. Little girls especially love to watch aspiring dancers in action. Our Girlfriend Lauren takes her son and horse-loving little girl to a stable about twenty minutes from her house so they can watch big kids ride and the unsaddled animals trot around the pasture.

SPORTING GOODS STORES: On a boring winter afternoon, your local sports equipment superstore is as good as an amusement park for many little boys and some very game girls. There's lots of space to run around, balls to play with, and major league paraphernalia to ogle. Dad will be happy as a clam, and if team sports don't blow your skirt up, you can check out the exercise clothes.

PLANT NURSERIES: On a not-too-hot, not-too-cold day, explore the greenhouses and growing sheds at a nearby plant place. If you want, pick out a simple flower, like a potted marigold, as a take-home token.

TOY STORES: Skip big, noisy superstores unless you are actually looking for a migraine. The smaller, boutiquey places tend to have cozy spots for the kids to play and a friendlier, quieter atmosphere. Do give the place your business when possible (ideally without small people in tow), but don't make a habit of buying stuff for your child every time you visit.

MUSICAL INSTRUMENT STORES: If you watch your children carefully so they don't do major demolition, these places are great. Walk around and check out the keyboards. Gently show your child how to bang on a drum, clang some cymbals, or shake a shakere. Frequently, these stores also sell nicer, simpler versions of the cheap plastic instruments you find at the toy store.

OUT-OF-THE-WAY PLAYGROUNDS: Instead of hitting the same playground all the time, check out different spots around town and elsewhere in your area. Sounds simple, but for some kids it's as good as stumbling on the Lost City of Atlantis. Stop at a new spot for a cold drink or treat when you're done.

LOCAL TRANSPORTATION: Our Girlfriend Diana took her boys for a big, action-packed day in the Big Apple. To this day, what they remember most is the bus ride there and back. It's a fact: Often times, kids love the "getting there" as much as the "there." So why not make that the main event? Hop on a train, take it a few stops to another town, and find a fun place to have lunch or eat a picnic. Our Girlfriend Lauren, who lives in New York, regularly rides with her kids on a commuter tram to a residential island in the middle of the East River. After a quick ice cream, they jump back on and soar back to Manhattan. A jaunt on the Staten Island ferry is another favorite.

OUTDOOR SCULPTURE GARDENS: This may sound esoteric, and we guess it is—if you think of sculpture as fine art. But if you look at this stuff through the unjaded eyes of a child—it's just pretty darned awesome. Think about it—enormous hulks made from mysterious metals and rocks looming up out of the ground. You've got huge electrical outlets and garden trowels by Claes Oldenburg, brightly hued hulks from Calder that look like Legos on steroids, and those cartoonlike cut outs from Keith Haring. Even if your child pays little attention to the art that's on display, he'll have lots of soft, well-manicured grass to run around on while you check it all out. Bring a picnic lunch and the day is made. Sculpture gardens and parks are often located on corporate campuses, at art museums, and at universities. For an international directory of what's out there, log on to www.sculpture.org. Botanical gardens are another excellent option along these lines. They tend to be more peaceful than plain old parks, and often feature wonderful seasonal events like chile pepper fiestas and cherry blossom festivals. For some of our urban Girlfriends, an afternoon jaunt to the local botanic garden has lulled cranky toddlers into a divine snooze alfresco.

THE WOODS: Grab your sports-utility stroller or a baby backpack and take on a woodsy trail with the little ones. (Of course, if you're going on your own, don't go anywhere too isolated.) It doesn't matter how far you get or if you reach any destination at all—if you've got a preschooler walking alongside you, you may only reach the first mud hole before he gets sidetracked and eventually realizes he's too tired to walk any farther. The point is that from a child's perspective, the woods themselves—any kind of woods—are filled with all sorts of fascinating stuff that's entertainment all on its own: gurgling brooks teeming with tiny fish, feathery ferns, fragrant pillows of puffy moss, lichen-coated bark. Bring water, snacks, sunblock, jackets, hats, and a resealable plastic bag so you can collect leaves for a collage-making session back home.

CHAPTER FOUR

Playdates

We've talked about setting up a house so it's fun and easy to live in with little kids. We've pinpointed which toys and play props really get the most mileage. We've shared lots of totally simple ways to do and make cool things with your mommy-infatuated darling. Now, the Girlfriends are going to toss yet another fun factor into the mix: other little people.

Not siblings, Girlfriend. Playdates—many children's first wobbly step on the road to sociability and many moms' best shot at getting some relief in the entertainment department. That's because even if a playdate takes place in your home and even if you must still supervise from the sidelines and perhaps hang out with the mommy who came along with your little visitor, there is at least some other person present who can distract (and perhaps delight) your child. Someone else is there and all too eager to dress up, empty and refill the same bucket of sand two hundred times, chase imaginary puppies through the house, or simply make fart sounds with his palms while you fold the wash or enjoy what it feels like to have your hiney touch a seat cushion for more than thirty seconds at a stretch. That's nothing to sneeze at.

The playdate payoff—for you and your child—isn't instant, nor does it come without effort, however. It takes time and some serious hand-holding on a caregiver's part before a child gets comfortable with the idea of separating and is actually capable of cavorting with people his own size. Exactly how much effort and how pleasant this process is, depends on your temperament and your child's, whether he has older siblings, and plain old luck with regard to the proximity of compatible playpals and what their respective mommies are like.

In *The Girlfriends' Guide to Toddlers,* we write a whole bunch about the dynamics and diplomacy of playdates. We talk about how to handle biters and boppers. We talk about loners and natural-born socialites. We talk about all the reasons why it's worth helping young kids cultivate friendships and some of the unexpected challenges you'll find on your mission. If—for some unimaginable reason—you haven't yet read the *Toddlers* book, go get it! Soak up what we have to say on the social life of young children, then pick up right here where you left off.

Now we're going to get a bit more specific. We want to get down to the nitty-gritty of what we think makes playdates work and what role we mommies should—and shouldn't—play in this whole social circus.

Motherhood: Your Passport Back to Social Insecurity

Yes, playdates can be a parent's salvation in many respects. But the issue of a child's developing social life—especially a firstborn's—is also rife with opportunities for insecurity and worry—for us moms, not our young children.

Very early on, we start hearing about all kinds of classes and play groups and wonder if maybe our babies "need" to be a part of the action. At some point—usually when preschool starts—we realize other children are developing their own set of buddies. We may be horrified to see "in" crowds and "out" crowds already starting to form. (What we don't realize is that many of those social butterflies we're seeing are younger siblings, who tend to sprout relationships like damp lawns grow mushrooms.) Now, in addition to juggling everything else, we feel pressure to start engineering the social life of a person who doesn't even know her own phone number.

Can you say angst? If a child's mommy isn't a personal friend of yours, you can actually feel nervous about calling and asking for a "date." Even worse, if she accepts, there's no guarantee the rendezvous will be a comfortable one. Our Girlfriend Kelly felt all kinds of pressure to set up playdates for her very shy son when he started preschool. He, however, had no interest in the matter whatsoever. Kelly ended up entertaining visiting moms and babes, while Max hid upstairs in his room or in a far-flung corner of the yard. She finally stopped torturing herself (and everyone else) and took a hiatus from the whole thing. Four months later, Max asked for his first playdate. Today, he's not the life of the party by a long shot, but he's got a few really good friends and they adore spending time together.

We're telling you this story right off the top because, as Girlfriends who are at least a little further along in this game, we can look back and truly say it's not worth getting uptight about your child's first steps as a social being. In the same way that they don't all figure out how to roll over or walk at the same age, children start clicking with other children at very different points and face wildly different challenges along the way. So stay calm about all this—especially if you're not a big joiner or don't have the opportunity to be. There are many ways to help a child get comfortable with other little people and they don't all involve sitting around a near stranger's basement on Tuesday mornings singing nursery rhymes with ten other moms. Above all, we want you to realize what we were only able to learn through our own well-intentioned blunders: **Your child is not you and she may have very different ideas about socializing.** Follow her lead and provide encouragement and support when you can. She may not turn out to be the Pearl Mesta of Paramus, but she'll be a whole lot happier if you don't force her to be someone she's not or to do things before she's ready. Now that we've made that clear, let's get started.

CHAPTER FIVE

The Mommy Date

Here's a basic truth most of us only realize in retrospect:

Babies don't need friends. Mommies do.

Children under the age of about two and a half aren't very discriminating when it comes to other small children. They're curious, but this social curiosity is more along the lines of "Oooh, he has hands, too" or "I want that muffin," as opposed to "I wonder which American League pitcher he likes the best." **Simply being around other little people and becoming familiar with them—regardless of their gender, political interests, or temperament (as long as they aren't uncontrolled biters or boppers)—is all the social exposure small children really need early on.**

Thus, trying to find your child the perfect playmates at this very early age is just plain misguided. Your mission—for your sake, and eventually for your child's—should be to find a mommy

Girlfriend (or Girlfriends) who's fun and easy to spend time with and who's available to hang out when you are. It helps if the kids are close in age, not for some lofty psychological reasons, but for basic practicality, since even a few months can make a huge difference as far as what a young child can and cannot do. It's not very social, for example, if you're sitting over at the sandbox with your not-yet-walking twelve-month-old and your mommy friend is stuck at the other end of the playground with her monkey-bar climbing eighteen-month-old.

In an ideal world, your mommy Girlfriends would be the Girlfriends you had before you gave birth. But since we can't all count on having babies at the same time, making the same career decisions, and settling down in the same place, lots of us have no choice but to sniff out some new company. At our advanced age, this can be pretty awkward. How to go about this without feeling like you're in seventh grade again?

SIGN UP FOR THOSE MOMMY AND ME CLASSES (FORCE YOURSELF IF YOU MUST). "Music for Everyone" and "Junior Gym" classes won't turn your infant or toddler into Yo-Yo Ma or Arnold Schwarzenegger. Lots of our little darlings actually spent a good part of their "class time" clinging to us for dear life. The point of these gigs is to get you and your babe out of the house and into the company of others who must also lug around large bags stuffed with diapers and whip out a breast or bottle on occasion. Unlike those postpartum support groups for moms, you won't get to chat up other mothers as much during these classes. (Some of us have actually gotten in trouble for talking. Yes, we're serious.) But classes are a pretty good place to plug into the mommy network and suss out who is around and what other family-friendly activities and organizations are in your area. The "Clay Play" crowd might not work for you or your child, but it could lead you to another group that does.

HANG OUT AT MAJOR MOM MAGNETS. You know how the guys in *Cheers* could just show up at the bar and count on running into at least a couple of their cronies? There are places like this for moms, too. For those of us like our gregarious Girlfriend Stacy—who can chat up just about anything with a pulse—these spots are key. Think local playground, Starbucks, any local bookstore that has a children's section. If you show up at around the same time every day or every week, you'll start recognizing faces and tots pretty quickly. Over time, you'll start chatting with someone—if only because your toddler has filched her child's doll stroller or spilled her iced latte. Stacy made sure to bring a big bucket of sidewalk chalk every time she went to the local playground with her daughter Jade. The chalk attracted other little kids like flies to orange soda—and lots of nice mommies came along. Even if you never get together with any of these characters at another location, the familiarity of the place and the people will be great for you and your little one.

JOIN A MOM GROUP OR PLAY GROUP. Lending credence to the phrase "safety in numbers," the natural hustle and bustle of group get-togethers tends to ease the intensity of mommy dating. There are at least a few people present to chat up, and awkward moments can always be escaped by chasing after a wayward child or popping up to help the host mom distribute bowls of Veggie Booty.

There are two basic types of groups you generally hear about—mother's groups and play groups. Mother's groups tend to draw moms of younger babies craving some company. What's nice about these gigs is that they are often offered by community centers and hospitals. There's no exclusivity or worry about being invited to participate—just pay a reasonable fee and you're in. There's a contingent of Girlfriends who met at their local Y's mom's group and they hit it off so well, they continued to get together long after the formal twelve sessions were finished. To this day—though they're all dispersed throughout the great suburbs of Chicago—several still get together with their growing broods on a monthly basis. Another group of young moms started an e-mail group based largely in New Jersey (although one Girlfriend has moved to Paris) with about forty members. They get together once a year for a picnic, but they talk *virtually* almost every day.

Then there are play groups. Most often organized by word of mouth, these tend to draw moms of older babies who are at least under the impression that their kids are going to play with each other. In reality, however, most moms go to play groups for the same reason they enroll in mom's groups: for company and some relief.

With this truth about play groups out on the table, the Girlfriends want to emphasize that your focus when searching for one should be on finding nice moms, not impressive agendas. Yeah, we've popped in on some homegrown play groups that really go all out—they have formal activities, complete with craft time, singing circles, and sign language lessons. Frankly, the Girlfriends just can't buy into that whole ultra-organized baby-focused scene. Contrary to what some play group gurus may contend, we believe that play groups *should* be a time for moms to hang loose a little and let their toddlers tussle among themselves nearby. Of course, we have to keep them from killing or eating each other and help put shy ones at ease. But as we've said before, it's just plain silly to make every action and interaction so forced and deliberate. Just being around each other is social exposure in itself.

How to find a play group? If you don't come upon one by word of mouth, you might check community bulletin boards to see if a group is seeking members. In the Girlfriends' experience, though, this "blind date" approach to play groups is the best way to end up in a stilted situation or on the fringe of some flock you have nothing in common with. (The organized mom's groups we discussed above are different since they often have a moderator and generally have a fixed start and finish date.) A better option is to try organizing a group yourself. Now, don't snort. We're not talking about creating a caucus here—a few moms is fine for starters. Ask a couple of moms in those baby music classes or at the playground if they're interested. Ring up some of the women you took a shine to at your postpartum support group. Chances are they might know someone who'd be game, too. It's like that old shampoo commercial—you'll tell two friends, and they'll tell two friends, and so on, and so on.

One more note on joining a mom's group or play group: It's not necessary that you adore or attach yourself to the whole gang. As our Girlfriend Lilo's grandmother said when Lilo complained about how many loser men there were at a Jewish singles party she forced herself to attend: "Who cares how many losers there were. One good one is enough." That's what happened to our Girlfriends Cynthia and Cathryn, who met in a play group they both turned out to abhor. While most of the other mothers chirped on about how great they were doing and how soundly their darlings were sleeping, Cynthia and Cathryn sat with their "spirited" toddlers wondering what mommy train they were on—since it sure wasn't delivering the same ride everyone else was having. At some point, they caught each other's eye mid-roll and knew they just had to talk. Before they knew it, they were attached at the hip—rescuing the tots from the monkey bars, groaning about sleep deprivation, and obsessing over when to wean and when to start potty training. Years later, who knows where those other moms are. But Cynthia and Cathryn are pregnant again and their firstborn are as close as siblings. Would you believe it—their hubbies adore each other, to boot. Some Girlfriends have all the luck.

Play Group Pointers

- **Create a roster.** This sounds formal, but it's really just practical. Circulate a list with everyone's name, the child's name and food allergies if any, phone number, address, and e-mail. This way, it's easy and comfortable for individuals to get in touch with each other without necessarily going through the group organizer.

- **Take a stance on sick kids.** Don't get militant about it, but do set a standard for what you're all comfortable with. Is a runny nose out of the question? Or only if the runny stuff is green? Decide on this together.

- **Make house rules clear.** If you're hosting, pipe up if you don't want kids eating on that new couch or wandering upstairs and out of bounds. If you spend your time biting your tongue and your nails, you'll just get bitchy.

- **Childproof the space.** Take all the obvious precautions. Move easily breakable stuff out of the way. If there are kids both above and below the choke hazard stage in the group, be safe and clear the deck of small pieces.

- **Keep pets out of the picture.** One Girlfriend's adorable boxer puppy may be another's nightmare of slobber. Avoid problems and tension—don't ask, just do it. Some children (and their parents) are afraid of animals, are allergic, or are concerned about animals who bite. Err on the side of caution here.

- **Put out limited—and appropriate—playthings.** Forget anything with lots of pieces or that requires intense parental supervision. This is the time for big, chunky trucks, push carts, balls, soft blocks, and dolls. Stow away and out of sight any favorite toys that your child won't want to share. If possible, provide doubles of the good stuff. A few hunks of

Play-Doh plopped on a table are great for encouraging cooperative play if you gather in a space that's mess-friendly. Bubbles are also an easy way to lure tots toward a common area.

- **Gather somewhere that's relatively confined.** A finished
  basement, a smallish fenced-in yard, the common room of
  an apartment building are all good choices. Otherwise, the
  toddlers will disperse like gas molecules and individual
  mommies will have no choice but to run right after them.

- **Don't go overboard with food.** If play group turns into a
  county cookoff, it'll become more burden than it's worth.
  Gather before or after lunch and put out simple snacks. If
  the location alternates between houses, hosts can provide
  food when it's their turn. Otherwise, everyone can bring a little something each week.

- **Keep it on the short side.** Since we're not big on rolling out
  an elaborate activity roster in order to keep the kids constantly busy, we say the whole gig should be up in less than
  two hours.

- **Don't get carried away.** As the Girlfriends see it, play groups
  are a way to meet some people, not a way of life or a career
  option. Keep it simple, let the kids grow accustomed to each
  other, and have some fun. If the group grows bored with the
  basic setup, don't drive yourself nuts trying to make the affair
  more exciting. You'll be much better off adapting the friendships you make to fit your evolving lifestyle. Get together for
  family barbecues, rent a beach bungalow together, or get
  those mommies out on their own and form a book club. With
  the right kind of nurturing, some of these friendships may
  end up lasting a lifetime.

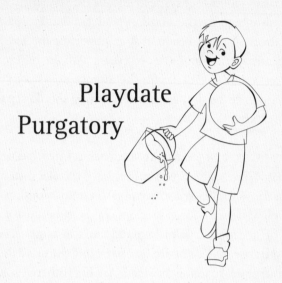

CHAPTER SIX

Playdate
Purgatory

The start of preschool is usually the start of what the Girl-friends call Playdate Purgatory. It is that time when kids start striking up friendships all their own—yet they're not quite ready to actually hang out with these buddies *on their own*. That of course means mommy must start spending time in the kitchens of complete strangers (and vice versa) while her precious child lays the foundation for lifelong friendships (ha). If you work all week, that might even mean that you have to do this on a precious Saturday or Sunday, while your hapless spouse heads to The Home Depot by himself. There really is no way to completely avoid this stage—but there are ways to accelerate the arrival of what you're all ultimately aiming for. That is, of course, the drop-off playdate. Our step-by-step strategy:

CUT YOUR TEETH WITH MOMMY GIRLFRIENDS OR BLOOD RELATIVES FIRST. It's tempting to stick around with your best mommy Girlfriends or your own sister when your respective babes are playing together. But take advantage of the comfort and familiarity. Make this your first drop-off relationship. It'll be easier for the kids, since they've already spent months or even years with the mommy and child in question. It'll be easier for the mommies—since you can trust each other to be simpatico and soothing should separating be dicey for starters.

WHEN YOU'RE READY TO TRY CLASSMATE PLAYDATES, LET YOUR CHILD CHOOSE HER COMPANY. Here's where you might have to take a step away from what drove those earlier attempts at companionship. Don't arrange a playdate with some random child just because you like the looks of her mother at pickup and don't instantly accept an invitation just because it's offered, either. Now the playdate really is about your child, so follow her lead. Ask her if there's someone in the class she'd like to have over. If she comes up with a blank or looks like you've just suggested that you all go to the pediatrician for a nice big penicillin shot, put the idea on a back burner for a while.

KEEP IT ONE ON ONE. Groups might be okay for toddlers, but they can be confusing and frustrating for preschoolers who are just learning how to form friendships. Even a group of three (known as the Bermuda Triangle) can leave someone feeling left out. It's also helpful if you can keep siblings—especially little ones—out of the fray.

MEET IN EACH OTHER'S HOMES. It might be more comfortable to meet somewhere neutral, like a playground or a padded cell that rents by the hour, and the kids might be less territorial about their stuff. But half of this drop-off game is getting children comfortable with their surroundings. So bite the bullet and kick off where the playdates are ultimately going to take place. This will also give you the chance to suss out if the host house is safe and if the folks who live in it seem relatively sane. When you get there, ask the host mom and child to show you where the bathroom is and where the kids are allowed to play. (Do hold off on asking if she keeps a loaded gun in her nightstand—it may be what's really on your mind but the question can be a bit off-putting.) If older sibs are in the house, get introduced so they don't seem scary to your little one. Check out the pet situation, too, and let the host mom know if large, black shaggy dogs tend to freak your child out. If that's the case, go ahead and ask if the pet can be kept out of the picture. Mention food allergies, too: Peanut sensitivities especially are nothing to laugh about. When it's your turn to host, do the same for your guests.

DON'T HOVER. Definitely help break the ice and get things going. Kick a ball around with the kids or check out the host child's amazing Barbie collection. Then try your best to step back, mom—unless someone's getting bitten, objects are being broken, or everything's melted down into a crying, whining mess. The longer you micromanage, the longer it will take for you to subtract yourself from the scene altogether.

FOCUS ON HOW MUCH, NOT HOW MANY. Don't get caught up in popularity contests. If you start scheduling playdates with every kid in the class, you'll end up sitting in strangers' kitchens until it's time for junior high. The goal here—for your child and for you—is reaching some level of comfort and familiarity. The best way to do that is to find a couple of compatible pals and arrange regular playdates with them. To a child—and to lots of us Girlfriends—a handful of familiar faces and places are worth a thousand fleeting friendships any day of the week.

THE DROP-OFF. There's no way to know for sure when your child is ready to go solo. Generally, though, when the kids are off and running within ten seconds of your arrival and they can go a good ten minutes without bellowing for you, it's okay to try. Don't do a disappearing act, however. The Girlfriends have all attempted to sneak out quietly and the tactic has almost universally backfired. Talk about a good fodder for future therapy. The Girlfriends have had far better luck sticking around until the kids were in a groove, casually mentioning we were running out for a short while, then scramming. Plan to stay away for about an hour the first time and be sure to give the host mom a phone number where you can be reached.

SUBSEQUENT DROP-OFFS. Once your little socializer gets into the swing of things, you may very well be able to drop her off at the home of other new playmates without even putting your car in park. Don't. If you do not personally know the parents, it's your duty as a conscientious and sufficiently paranoid mommy Girlfriend to get your butt through the door and inside the house of every first-time playdate until your child herself absolutely forbids you from doing so. (At that point, you will have to find other sneaky ways of assessing how and where she is spending her time. Like selling Mary Kay cosmetics door-to-door or driving a UPS truck.) If you work during the week, schedule a first-time playdate with new pals on a weekend day so you'll be available.

All of this sounds simple—and it very well may be if your child's playmate is his family's firstborn. That mommy will most probably be right in step with you and urge you to come on in until the children get settled and it seems clear that no one is going to melt down. At least not immediately. If, however, your child's playmate is a younger sibling, you might be greeted by a perfectly lovely person who has absolutely no intention of spending any part of her afternoon with you. Your encounter might go something like:

YOU, STANDING BEHIND YOUR CHILD, YOUR HANDS FIRMLY PLANTED ON HIS SHOULDERS: Hi, I'm Trixy Slater. Here's Ethan—we've heard a lot about Herman. Ethan's so excited about this playdate. And um . . .

VETERAN MOM, STANDING RIGHT SMACK IN THE MIDDLE OF THE FRONT DOORWAY, FEET NOT BUDGING: Nice to meet you, I'm Betty. So, OK! C'mon Ethan. The kids are out back. Does five sound good, Trixy?

YOU: Uh, yeah! I think it should be . . .

VETERAN MOM, YELLING INTO THE HOUSE: I'll be there in a second! So we'll see ya then. I'll call you if there's any problem. Bye!

As we said, this veteran mommy is probably a completely excellent person and parent. It's just that she's done this playdate thing so many times—and she has so many playdates to keep track of—that she's probably forgotten how nerve-racking it can be in the beginning.

What you need to do is work quickly. Right after you introduce yourself to that mom, hand her a piece of paper with phone numbers of where you can be reached. Tell her if your child has any allergies she needs to know about. If you absolutely can't tolerate junk food, let your host know. But pick your prohibitions carefully—you want your child to feel comfortable and she might have a problem doing so if everyone else is eating Pop-Tarts and she's nibbling on low-sodium rice cakes. There's no telling where the line should be drawn here. It's one of those tough balancing acts you'll have to feel out for yourself as you go.

Your next bold step is to say firmly but nicely (assuming your host isn't inviting you in and chatting up a storm herself) that you'd love to be able to help settle Ethan in and make sure he's comfortable before you leave. Tell the veteran playdate mom that if she's busy, you'll be perfectly fine hanging with the guys for few minutes on your own and that you'll pop your head in to say good-bye before you take off. Unless this mom is running a secret gambling operation, she will probably love you for doing this and run back into the kitchen to finish preparing dinner. Of course, while you are helping to break the ice with the guys, you will be using this opportunity to check out the place for free-floating knives and machetes, large rodents that aren't pets, and just an overall vibe that things are okay. If you do get a bad feeling, use our Girlfriend Maryann's strategy: Find the mom, put a stricken look on your face and blurt out, "I'm so embarrassed! I completely spaced it but Ethan has a dentist appointment that started ten minutes ago. Would you forgive us?" Make your exit quickly. If veteran mom calls for a playdate at her house again—and if your little Ethan adores her little Herman—simply say Ethan seems to do a little better when the playdates are at your house. We're betting she won't have a problem with that. If you don't like the Herman scene as a whole, just deflect any requests for future playdates until the drift is gotten. Chances are you will not have to do any of this, but it's a good card to keep in your deck.

One last note: Yes, playdates can provide you with a welcome respite. Yes, you might feel compelled to schedule them because all the other kids are trotting off with each other after school. Keep in mind, though, that above all, playdates are for your child. Make sure the playdates you're arranging are appropriate for her, not just convenient for you. And don't overschedule—kids have very busy, long days and they need the chance to kick back at home without a continuation of the chaos. Most of the Girlfriends have found that one or two playdates a week is more than sufficient to keep everyone happy.

Just the Three of Us

Now it's time for you to play host, Girlfriend. The first thing you should do is make the mommy who is dropping off her precious child feel free to breathe. You will do this by:

- Being warm and welcoming to her child the minute you set eyes on her.

- Asking that mom in, showing her and her darling around, requesting mom's phone number, asking if there are any foods or activities that are out of bounds, telling her if you have a pet and offering to lock it up somewhere if it would make her child more comfortable, and—if you are privileged enough to have a pool—telling mommy that said pool is fully fenced in and stays locked at all times. (Which of course it will be, right?)

As for what you are going to do once that mommy takes her exit, here's the Girlfriends' official answer: Not much.

The main point of a playdate is to give your child an opportunity to forge her own friendships. You ultimately won't be doing her any favors if you've got your big fat nose in the picture the whole time—no matter how charming or fun you may be. You also won't be doing yourself any favors since, as we said earlier in this chapter—playdates are a chance for mommy to get some sort of a break.

Your level of involvement will ultimately depend upon the age of the kids, their temperaments, and how they respond to each other. In general though, the progression should go something like this:

HELP BREAK THE ICE. If this playdate is taking place with children under the age of about three and a half, you'll have to stick pretty close because essentially you'll be quasi-baby-sitting your guest. Playpals this age are usually pretty happy potching around together (or in parallel) with toys in the playroom or rooting around in a sandbox. Dig in with them at first, then as they get comfortable, take this opportunity to kick back and monitor from the sidelines. If you are hosting older playpals and they have already disappeared to some fun corner of the house by the time you close the front door, pop in and see what the vibe is like. Let them know about any ground rules—"You must put the toy you are playing with away before you take out a new one" is a goodie. So is, for example, "No torturing younger siblings," "Mom's room is out of bounds," and "All doors stay open unless you are using the bathroom." If the kids are already in the throes of a major chess game (ha) go ahead and take your exit, letting them know where you'll be. If they seem at loose ends, go ahead and get them started with something. Set up some Play-Doh, pull the Lincoln Logs out and help them lay the castle foundation, bring the kids down to the playroom and show them where the dress-up clothes are. Then scram.

CHECK-IN. If you are hosting slightly older children and thus may not have them in your sight the entire time, don't assume that if you don't hear screaming or howling, everything's going ducky. Our Girlfriend Portia (who is really, truly a most diligent mom) made that mistake when her kindergartner, Alex, had his neighborhood pal Jonah over one afternoon. She only discovered there was a problem when Jonah's mom called, not-so-delicately inquiring why Jonah was playing alone in her backyard. Portia found Alex watching MTV in the master bedroom. Apparently, there had been some disagreement between the two gentlemen as to what they wanted to do that day. A word to the wise: Always be suspicious if things are *too* quiet.

Granted, not all mishaps are this extreme. The point is that children—especially young ones—can lose their way during a playdate pretty quickly. It's important for you to check in frequently and if the kids seem bored or about to beat each other up, redirect what they're doing. If matters are really getting rough—if the two are fighting or simply not interacting—it's time for you to get more involved and to introduce some new, possibly mom-monitored activities. See our section on Playdate SOS Strategies.

SERVE A SNACK. Round up the troops and roll out some eats. It's a great way to calm kids down, bring them together, and get to know your visitor a bit better. No need to serve anything elaborate, though our Girlfriend Jill has won over countless kiddie visitors by always having a can of spray whipped cream in the fridge. Whether she uses it to top a scoop of ice cream, a couple of ripe strawberries, or heck—a Nilla wafer—that can of cream seems to turn even the dullest playdate into an event. Same goes for cool ice cream accoutrements like cones, sprinkles, and colored sugar—even if you're serving them with frozen nonfat yogurt.

Here's a great game to play while the kids are snacking (or any time you all want to get better acquainted): What Do You Like Better? Start firing off all kinds of questions along these lines—What do you like better, peas or broccoli? French fries or ice cream? Popcorn or pretzels? Arthur or SpongeBob? Baseball or football? Liver or brussels sprouts? McDonald's or Burger King? Believe it or not, kids really feel important when adults want to know this stuff. They can't wait to answer—and their answers naturally spark up conversation and friendly controversy between them. You the mom will get to know what your guest will and won't eat, what this individual thinks is fun, how often his parents buy him fast food, and lots of other stuff you might not have the nerve to ask his parents directly.

GIVE FAIR WARNING. Let the little buddies know that the playdate will be ending in ten minutes or so and that it's time to start cleaning up. It's perfectly okay for you to help them do so, but make sure they participate. If there's a meltdown about the impending demise of their rendezvous, do your best to get the kids out of the room they're playing in and into more neutral territory—like the kitchen. Give them some juice, chat about the next playdate and what they might want to do, and bound for the door when mom arrives. If you, like our Girlfriend Shelli, end up in a situation where moms are chronically late for pickup, take the bull by the horns at the start of the playdate and offer to take your little guest home yourself. Think in terms of two hours, max.

'FESS UP TO EVERYTHING. If your child and his playdate walk in on you while you're on the toilet (which happened to our Girlfriend Helen) . . . if your little guest gets so much as a mosquito bite while he's in your care . . . if your child was an absolute tyrant the entire afternoon . . . go ahead and tell mom when she comes for pickup. The last thing you'll want is for your little visitor to transmit the information to his mom and have her up in arms that "Evan's mom was marching around nude at four o'clock in the afternoon," or that "Evan So-and-so is a holy terror and his mother doesn't do anything about it." Even if your visitor doesn't say anything, you'll never be quite sure and might wonder if that's why his mom is looking at you funny.

SAY CIAO! Make sure your pint-size host gets into the habit of seeing his friend to the door. Even if it means retrieving him from his room and instructing him to say good-bye—while his guest and his mommy stand waiting at the front door—it's a lesson that's got to be learned. Chances are that mommy will more than understand what you are trying to accomplish.

SOS: How to Rescue a Playdate

- Your four-year-old daughter and her friend have played for fifteen minutes of a two-hour playdate. Your guest appears in the kitchen and declares she wants to go home because your child won't let her play with any of her Barbies. When you go upstairs to troubleshoot, you find your daughter in one heck of a mood and realize this ain't going anywhere good.

- Your six-year-old son and his buddy are playing T-ball. Every time your fiercely competitive child tags his guest "out," your guest starts yelling "No fair, you cheated!" After a few rounds with you trying to play ump, the boys are about to blow.

- Your child and his guest act as if they don't know each other.

- You have a shy or socially uncomfortable child. She wants to have a playdate but is terrified.

Welcome to great moments in playdate history. It's times like these where you've got to stick more than your toes or your nose in to salvage the situation. Here are some cool activities and tactics that have worked very well for the Girlfriends:

Change the Scene

If the kids are tussling over T-ball in the backyard, bring them inside and take out the Legos. If the girls are fighting over who gets to be which Groovy Girl, leave the dolls behind and set up some crafts in the kitchen or playroom (see Simple Crafts section on page 50 for ideas). Move tiffing toddlers out of the toy room, settle down somewhere cozy with one on either side of you, and read a couple of books. If there is general mayhem because no one is willing to share anything, take the kids (with the other mom's permission) to neutral territory, like a local playground or to town for hot chocolate or a cold drink and to throw pennies in the fountain outside the savings bank.

Serve a Snack

As we said, a snack is a great way to change gears and take play-dates down a notch. If the kids really need some extra supervision and conciliation, turn snack into an activity. Make smoothies, bake some cookies, or just let them pick out a couple of different dry cereals to make their own snack mix.

Conjure Up a Cooperative Project

PAINT A BOX. Haul the biggest box you can find out of your recycling pile, put the kids in smocks or old T-shirts, and let them go crazy painting the thing. Have them do it on a plastic tarp in the yard, driveway, or, in the winter, the basement.

CHALK UP THE DRIVEWAY. Give them the sidewalk chalk and see what they scribble, or help them trace the outlines of each other's body (or yours) with the chalk and draw in the details. Older kids can play hopscotch, that old chestnut, or play Hangman out-of-doors.

PAINT WITH WATER. Fill a couple of plastic containers with water, get out some old foam or bristled house painting brushes and tell the kids you need some portion of the (house, deck, fence) "painted." Sounds hokey but for kids under about five this Tom Sawyer tactic works like a gem. Of course, make it clear only water should be used unless you want your house looking like a Jackson Pollock painting.

WASH THE CAR. We've already extolled the virtues of this. It's a sure bet when the weather is warm.

Do Something Outrageous

A few winters ago, our Girlfriend Margot was faced with a dull November day and two kindergarten boys who were about to drive her into an early grave. The boys had taunted Margot's youngest son, Noah, to the point where the little guy took a nice, healthy bite out of the playmate's left arm. The playmate responded by jumping on Noah's *Bob the Builder* video. Margot's older boy Ben got furious at Garrett because he happened to like *Bob the Builder,* too. At her wit's end, Margot hauled the family's plastic swimming pool out from winter storage and put it right outside the back door. As she made trips back and forth to the kitchen sink, filling the pool up with very warm water and bubble bath, she called Garrett's mom for permission to let the guys take a winter "swim." Being a laid-back Girlfriendly type, Garrett's mom gave the thumbs-up. Then Margot called the boys—who were fighting about something new upstairs. When they caught sight of the pool—frothing over with bubbles, the steam rising up into the cool but not-too-chilly air, the bathing suits set out on the ground—they couldn't move fast enough. The sheer outrageousness of a winter swim replaced any thoughts about bite marks or broken videotapes. The three kids spent the rest of the afternoon splashing in the tub, hooting and hollering, and begging Margot to ferry in fresh batches of warm water. It was a memorable playdate that turned into a tradition and it helped seal an important friendship for Ben and Garrett (not to mention Margot and Garrett's mom, Lisa).

Along these same lines, put the kids in cruddy clothes and let them get muddy and messy out in the rain (with mom's permission, of course). Put on your manicurist hat and give your daughter and her playdate matching manicures (make sure it's okay with mom if you don't know her very well). The idea is to introduce a shared, noncompetitive activity that is so completely kooky or just plain tempting, the kids can't help but delight in it together.

Discipline Delicately

Of course, you should let your guest know—and remind your child—what the basic rules are in your house and that you expect them to be followed. What happens, though, when they're not? Theoretically you could be a hard-ass and send your own child or his guest for a time-out when there's a problem. But in reality, the Girlfriends have saved this or any other form of rigid discipline for extreme occasions, such as big-time hitting, destructiveness, or unbearable rudeness. This is a playdate after all—you are dealing with someone's child other than your own and you don't need your home to become a stage for conflict resolution. Our Girlfriend Maryann takes a more low-key approach when her high-spirited son Gabriel and his equally combustible best buddy

Zack come to fisticuffs. She breezily announces it's time for the two to take a "time-out from each other," and sends them off to play separately until the two boys show evidence that they've calmed down. It spares any single individual humiliation or blame and lets both of them calm down and regroup.

Get Out the Electronics

The Girlfriends don't generally believe that playdates are a great time for TV or computers. When all else fails, however, and we simply don't want to make a scene by calling mom for an early pickup, we've been known to knuckle under. Sometimes good buddies simply need that break, especially toward the end of a playdate. Sometimes, a movie is what will get us through a mismatched situation. For example, if you host a new playmate who is absolutely miserable and refuses to do anything you've suggested, why subject your own child to further shenanigans? The opposite is also true. Turn on the tube or the computer, let the time pass, usher your guest out the door, and move on. Believe us, Girlfriend, you'll have plenty more opportunities to get this playdate thing down. Ultimately, all of this will be worth the effort. You'll soon be begging your child to bring her friends home so you can see what kind of humans she's hanging out with and the best way to succeed is to make your house a place where your children and their friends feel happy spending their time. As we see it, it's never too early to start.

What If Mom Works?

For those of us who work outside the home, the word "playdate" has very different implications. If our children are in group day care, the term may be altogether off the radar, since every day is essentially an ongoing playdate. If our children are cared for by a baby-sitter, a playdate is usually something the baby-sitter sets up so she can hang out with other baby-sitters.

If our children are in school, playdates are something they ask for but we feel nervous and guilty about—either because it's something we can't easily or possibly arrange for them or because we don't like the idea of them going off unescorted to the homes of people we really don't know.

What's a working mom to do in the latter situation? As our Girlfriend Kate learned, trying to get your child together with his friends on the weekend isn't a very realistic option since many families seem to have an unofficial "no playdates" rule for Saturdays and Sundays. What you can do, though, is schedule the initial playdate for the weekend, explaining to the mom that you work and that you'd simply like this chance for everyone to get acquainted. If everyone hits it off, then explore your options for get-togethers during the week. If your child is in an after-school program, the other mom may very possibly be happy to sign her out with your permission once a week or every other week. You may not be able to return the exact same favor. But you could, like Kate does, offer to have the playpal over on the occasional Saturday or Friday evening so that her mommy can have a night out.

If your child has an afternoon baby-sitter, offer to send your sitter along on the playdate so she can help out. After a few visits, (if both mom and baby-sitter are comfortable with the idea) your child's friend may very well be able to visit your house after school while the baby-sitter is in charge. (You will quickly observe that baby-sitters would rather do almost anything than hang out with a "mom." That includes watching an extra, unescorted child.)

Whatever you do, don't beat yourself up about the effect your work has on your child's playdate schedule. Don't forget, your child is seeing other kids all day at school. Cultivate relationships with cousins and neighbors—who are generally easier to access on the weekends. Put her in an after-school activity if you want. If your child has a formal "playdate" even once every two weeks, it'll be plenty.

Part 2

Parties:
The Mother of All
Fun Occasions

Top Ten Birthday Party Blunders

10. Taking twenty six-year-olds to Chuck E. Cheese's and not requiring that they all wear Day-Glo hats or T-shirts to make them stand out in the crowd.

9. Letting very small people "help" pull the candles out of the cake right after they've been blown out—*ouch!*

8. Not separating the kids well enough at the candle blow-out to ensure that some big ol' six-year-old doesn't spit all over the candles and cake before your little darling has had a chance to purse her lips.

7. Forcing your child to sit on Bart Simpson's lap when he won't even take his hands down from over his terrified eyes. Can you say, "Wet lap for Bart?"

6. Believing that your toddler will be so excited about her birthday that she won't even notice she's missing her nap.

5. Neglecting to tell all parents at a drop-off party that at party's end, all leftover children will be dropped at the local Y.

4. Insisting that grandparents and other dignified people attend theme birthday parties, where they will be silly-stringed and passed a yellow boa constrictor from the Reptile Man.

3. Picking a fight with daddy because he doesn't seem to be as effusive and energetic as you.

2. Letting the party kids open the birthday presents as a sort of free-for-all. They will either break, steal, or weep over the loss of each and every one, plus they'll separate the card from the gift and thank-you's will be a combination of fake outs and feeble memories.

1. Opening any envelopes that might contain money or gift certificates while opening the party gifts. Collect all cards from money and certificate-givers and put them in your drawer until the mayhem has calmed or else they will all be thrown away with the wrapping paper and dirty cake plates.

CHAPTER SEVEN

Popping the Birthday Party Bubble

Ancient societies made big sacrifices for their royal birthday celebrations. We've all seen footage of the fetes Hollywood starlets threw for their pin-curled cuties. ("No wire hangers!") The Girlfriends truly wonder, though, when it became an imperative for normal Joes like us to go completely nuts over what was once considered a basic backyard event.

After years of getting sucked up by the insanity of the Overblown Birthday—or making apologies because we can't or won't keep up with it—the Girlfriends think it's about time someone added some down-in-the-trenches perspective to the party picture. And who's better suited for the job than a bunch of veterans like us? We don't own glue guns. Our parties haven't been featured in major magazines. But we've staged and attended oodles and oodles of these shindigs—from folksy homespun get-togethers to off-premise rent events—and we know what works, what's really mattered to our kids, and what was simply a big fat waste of time, energy, and/or bucks. As good, devoted Girlfriends, we want to share what we've learned with you.

Let us get started by setting the record straight about what a real-life birthday party *does not*, in fact, need to be. Contrary to what all those party books and party pundits might imply or outright say:

IT DOES NOT HAVE TO BE REMEMBERED FOREVER. Talk about pressure! Think back to your childhood. What were birthdays like for you? Among the Girlfriends there definitely are those of us who remember special birthdays from our younger years. There are also plenty of us who couldn't provide a detail about their fourth bash, or for that matter, their fourteenth. As far as we can see, there ain't no correlation between who got the best parties and who ended up in therapy. Of course, our kids have home videos to refresh their memories, so feel free to edit out anything you don't want being discussed with a therapist in twenty years.

IT DOES NOT HAVE TO BE THE ULTIMATE STATEMENT ABOUT WHO YOU ARE AND THE PLACE YOU HOLD IN THE UNIVERSE. Even the most self-actualized, self-assured among us Girlfriends is willing to admit that we certainly do care about what parents think—however fleetingly—as they pull away from our children's birthday parties. It's nice to hear from a guest mom that the theme was adorable. It's great to know that the entertainment was—well—entertaining. But keep things in perspective here, Girlfriend. If you decide to let someone else do the work, nobody worth her salt will conclude that you're a lazy mother. If you do everything yourself, right down to the hand-sliced organic potato chips, few of us will decide that you are, officially, a superior breed. It's a child's party, after all, not your yearly debut. If you're gunning for feedback along the lines of "outrageous," "spectacular," or "remarkable," you might want to reconsider who you're putting this party on for and think about other ways of rounding out your personal profile.

IT DOES NOT HAVE TO BE THE MOST ORIGINAL IDEA IN THE WORLD. Certainly, kids do get sick of visiting the same indoor play zone Saturday after birthday Saturday. So do we parents. That doesn't mean you have to drive yourself batty drumming up some never-been-done concept. If your daughter fell in love with some clown she saw at her friend's party, go ahead and hire that character if that's what she wants and it fits your budget. You can find other ways to personalize the party—one of which will simply be that you'll be there enjoying Clover the Clown with her.

IT DOES NOT HAVE TO BE PERFECT. "Perfect birthday party," a phrase you'll find in many birthday books, is an oxymoron. As the Girlfriends have said countless times before, parenthood and childhood are messy business and "perfect" isn't part of the vocabulary. Cakes do go crashing to the floor, children fight, entertainers show up late and, in the case of our Girlfriend Helen's hired clown, stone-cold drunk. No matter how carefully you plan, a sudden storm can still wash out your backyard beach bash . . . your toddler can cry inconsolably from the moment your guests walk through the door . . . your grade-schooler's best buddy can fail to show and your birthday boy may then proceed to mope through the rest of the bash. *It's not the end of the world.* We have the rained-out birthday party photos and relatively well-adjusted children to prove it.

Now, here's the _truth_. A child's birthday party needs to be:

1. A fun way for your child to celebrate his day.

2. An event that is realistic, affordable—and perhaps enjoyable — for mommies and / or daddies to pull off.

3. Something with a clearly defined beginning and end. The middle is always up for grabs.

Period.

Without further ado, let us share what we've learned about accomplishing all three sanely and simultaneously.

The Girlfriend Game Plan

To Party or Not to Party, That *Is Still* the Question

What? No cake? No candles?

Hang onto your party hat, Girlfriend. Of course you should *celebrate* your babies' birthdays. These are among the great moments in a parent's life. (Along with that day our offspring inform us they want to make their own breakfast.) The Girlfriends are just saying that there's no dire need to start throwing full-blown birthday bashes right from year one or even two—a parenting loophole most of us Girlfriends only became aware of once we had our second and third kids.

Until children are *at least* three or four, and they start forging their own friendships, they will be pleased—*or displeased*—with whomever comes to celebrate their birthday with them. That includes grandma and grandpa, that includes a couple of kids from next door, that includes your best Girlfriends and the babies and spouses they drag along. So if you personally do not have the energy to brush your own hair, much less throw a soiree at this point in your motherhood adventure, don't sweat it. Tie some helium balloons to the back of a chair, invite a couple of key players with whom you would like to share the event (or who would be utterly offended if they were excluded), and have them help blow out the candles. It really can be that simple. The party police will not come after you, Girlfriends' honor.

The Other Party to Consider

Once you decide *you* are, indeed, up for throwing a party, it's time to think about what your *child* is up for. Sounds like an obvious thing, but the Girlfriends are going to go ahead and say what many folks won't admit: It is so, so easy to get carried away with planning a birthday party and completely overlook the needs and wants of your very own child. We've done it—not because we're selfish, horrible moms but because (a) these events seem to take on a life of their own and (b) when our children are young, we constantly underestimate how much they are aware of and how powerful their sentiments and opinions can be. So take these words to heart:

**Plan the party *with* your child—or at least—
with your child in mind.**

In the case of a child under three, truly consider his temperament. If he cowers around crowds and cries uncontrollably every time an unfamiliar adult enters the house, why torture him and everyone else by drumming up a big bash and blurting out every five minutes to your guests that "Nikki never cries like this, I think she must be teething!" We have a Girlfriend, Sally, who threw such a big bash for her first child's first birthday that for the next several years the little one screamed hysterically anytime anyone sang the Birthday Song.

Our advice: Do something small and revisit the idea next year.

Once you're dealing with a preschooler or grade-schooler, it's important to consider what your birthday child actually wants. However, don't blithely throw the "What would you like for your party?" question out there. Too many choices will likely over-whelm your little one and leave you trying to stage a medieval jousting match or bribing Michael Jordan to shoot hoops in your backyard. Think in terms of guided compromise. Ask your kindergartner if she'd like a princess party or a Powerpuff Girls party at home, for example. She may announce she actually wants to take her whole class to see the Powerpuff Girls movie. If that's not feasible, you might suggest that she pick three close buddies to take to the flick and follow up with ice cream and cake back home. A deal is made.

In case you don't put much stock in what we're saying about cooperative birthday planning, consider this cautionary little tale: When our Girlfriend Margot put down a deposit at a bowl-ing alley for her son's fifth birthday it seemed like the perfect idea for a December party—it was relatively affordable, it was sporty, and it was indoors but not in her house. Perfect, that is, unless you were the birthday boy, who announced shortly after hearing the news that he didn't want a bowling party and that—in fact—he hated bowling. Margot simply dismissed Ben's response, figur-ing he wasn't familiar with the sport. She sent out the invitations anyway. Over the coming weeks, Margot and her husband schlepped Ben and his little brother to the bowling alley, trying to build up Ben's confidence and enchant him with the sport. They ate soggy pizza together, watched the big guys bowl strikes, and learned how to keep score. Two weeks before the big day, Ben still insisted he didn't want a bowling party. Margot got mad. "Hey, I'm not going to force a child to have a party. He can have a bowling party or nothing!" When Ben heard his options, he chose the latter. That night, feeling pretty awful, Margot crept into Ben's room and asked him why he hated bowling so much. His answer nearly killed her. Turns out that Ben's very bestest pal, Jacob, said he wouldn't be able to go if the party was at a bowling alley. "Why?" Margot asked. "Because Jacob's mom said that the cigarette smoke at the bowling alley isn't good for his asthma. And if Jacob can't come, I don't want a party." If there had been a hair shirt in the nearest closet, Margot would have put it on and worn it for the rest of the year. Instead, she woke up early the next morning, asked Ben what he wanted to do for his birthday (his answer: a soccer party in the backyard, even though it was December), and spent the next six days hunting down a college soccer player to coach and praying it wouldn't snow. Ben and Jacob and their friends had a great—if chilly—time. Margot, though she nearly had a nervous breakdown, never loved her child more. There's a moral there. The Girlfriends beg you to heed it.

As for all the details—the invitations, the favors, the decorations, the activities. Include your child when possible, but don't beat yourself up if you simply don't have the time or opportunity to involve him in everything. For many of us, birthday parties—out of necessity—are put together in the wee hours after everyone is off to sleep. Or on borrowed time in the office. That's reality and it's okay! Tackle what you can, when you can, and keep your child posted as you go. There'll be plenty to do—and get excited about—together when the big day finally approaches.

Now, Get That Ball Rolling. As Soon As Possible

The Girlfriends aren't asking you to spend months on end actually planning your child's party. There are other things in life to get neurotic about. A few well-placed phone calls and Internet orders ahead of time, however, can lower your stress quotient, save money, and ensure that you get who and what you want for the B-day.

Here's how the Girlfriend Party Planning Time Line breaks down:

☐ **EIGHT WEEKS OR MORE:** If you are hiring entertainment or want to reserve a particular party location, it's almost never too early to make the call. Some super-popular options book prime time slots months in advance. Get confirmation *in writing*.

☐ **FIVE WEEKS:** Call key party invitees (even if that simply includes grandma and your child's best friend) and nail down a date. If you are putting on the party yourself, come up with a theme that's exciting for your child and reasonable for you to tackle. Write up a guest list.

☐ **FOUR WEEKS:** Prepare and send out invitations. Create a basic outline/schedule for the party. Write up a list of supplies you'll need for activities, projects, and the menu. Pinpoint sources for supplies—if using the Internet or catalogues, find out how long shipping will take (without incurring eleventh hour FedEx charges), then add three days.

☐ **TWO WEEKS:** Call invitees who haven't RSVP'd. We're not being presumptuous here but you'll need time to buy your supplies—especially if you're having a home party and you are ordering by mail. Purchase favors and supplies. Order birthday cake and/or food if you will not be making it yourself.

☐ **ONE WEEK:** Prep favors. Put together any props or project materials you'll be using. Clear and childproof space for the party; map out what will take place where. Buy food, except delicate last-minute stuff like mesclun lettuce and shrimp (gotcha). If you are holding the party outside your home or have hired help or entertainment, call and touch base. Do a dry run with your child/children and hubby of games and projects you have planned. Check out camera equipment, buy film, batteries, if necessary.

☐ **DAY BEFORE PARTY:** Prepare food, if advance prep is possible (which it should be). Bake birthday cake, if you are making it yourself. Set up and decorate the party space.

☐ **DAY OF PARTY:** Give your birthday child a hug and get ready for the big day. Finish food prep. Pick up food or cake, if you have placed orders, or send a Girlfriend. Finish last-minute decorations. Set up activity areas with appropriate materials. Buy ice, if necessary. Set table. Prep cameras. Action!

Tip: Our Girlfriend Cynthia starts off party day by giving her birthday baby some small "birthday" token he or she can wear around. It could be a paper crown, a #1 Birthday Kid badge made from cardboard, a cape, etc. It's a visual cue that reminds Cynthia, her birthday child, and everyone else, who the center of attention should be. (Eventually, kids will feel "too old" for this tradition. Cynthia assures us that yours will make their sentiments known when that moment does arrive.)

CHAPTER NINE

What a Difference a Day (and Date and Time) Makes . . .

Obviously, a birthday party should take place somewhere around the time of your child's actual birth date, but there is considerable flexibility here. Our Girlfriend Nancy, for example, regularly holds her son Thomas's party a month before his July 6 birthday. This way, he can celebrate with his friends before school is out. Likewise, if the magician your child has her heart set on gives you the choice between an awkward time slot on the weekend (like 9:30 A.M.) nearest your child's birthday or an excellent availability a week after that, take the latter. We've found that since we inevitably celebrate the actual birth day with our children, they don't get real picky about when the party happens.

The Dish on the Day of the Week

The best day of the week for birthday parties depends upon where you live. (Do teams have games on Saturdays? Are people big churchgoers? Do a lot of moms work full time?) It also depends on how old your child and her friends are, and how many people you want to actually turn out. So it's important to check out your individual situation before you blithely accept the first opening the Clownarium offers up. To give you an idea of how the various options tend to break down, here's what the Girlfriends have found.

WEEKDAY PARTIES. Weekdays are an okay time for a small, low-key party, especially for very young children. You face little, if any, chance that your young guests will show up with both parents tagging along (which minimizes what you'll have to do to keep the grown-ups amused). Some young children may actually come with their baby-sitters, which is great. Do keep in mind that if your child and her guests are in nursery school, you'll have to schedule the party in the afternoon to avoid conflicts with various school schedules—and kids can get cranky as the day wears on. Girlfriends who work full time point out that weekday parties can be problematic. If our children are in day care, if our baby-sitters don't drive, or if our grade-schoolers are in after-school programs, we've either gotta pass on these invitations (and have our kids feel left out of the fun) or take off from work (which, obviously, isn't always easy or even possible).

SATURDAY. Saturday is the unofficial "Birthday Day." We parents are generally running around doing errands and tend to factor parties into our to-do list as a matter of course. Just remember, everyone else will have the same idea about Saturday birthdays, so get those invitations out early (six weeks isn't out of the question). If your child or her friends are already playing team sports, schedule your party around the time when most Saturday games are played. If sports go all day in your town, you may be better off partying on Sunday. Also keep in mind, some folks have religious services on Saturday mornings.

SUNDAY. For some families, Sunday is a day they like to spend together. Our Girlfriend Jamie—whose husband travels extensively during the week—flat out declines all Sunday birthday party invitations, unless the guest of honor is a blood relative. Nevertheless, lots of us who work full time have no choice but to schedule parties on Sundays, since we need Saturday to pull everything together. The best way we've found to encourage attendance and keep parental noses in joint is to make the event a family-friendly affair. That means scheduling it after church hours and well before dinnertime. Those of us who live in areas where Sunday has a particularly strong "family vibe" tend to address the invitation to the guest and his family, and we set up the party accordingly. That means refreshments for parents and goody bags for siblings who tag along (there's nothing wrong with asking if siblings will be coming when a parent RSVP's). Many parents don't take us up on the offer, but those who have a Family Sunday tradition have always appreciated the gesture.

NAIL DOWN THE DATE. Before we send out any invitations, the Girlfriends generally pick out a couple of dates that will work for us. Then we pinpoint guests on the list who are absolute or near absolute musts—this might include cousins and grandparents if we are inviting family; this definitely includes our birthday child's very best couple of friends. Then we get on the horn and suss out which date works for the most guests on that short list. When we have that answer, we ring or e-mail back and ask those folks to mark their calendar—*in blood*. We then follow up with invitations—for them and the rest of the children on the guest list. Of course, ear infections and viruses can always happen (and they generally do), but this strategy at least minimizes the potential for schedule conflicts and major disappointments. One more important point: Check your child's class list early in the year to see if any students have a birthday that's near your child's. If so—and the kids travel in the same social circle or the school has an "all-or-nothing" policy about inviting fellow classmates to parties—be sure to ring up the other mom well in advance to coordinate the parties so they don't conflict. By the way, if your child's school doesn't have an "all-or-nothing" policy, here's what we recommend: Your child can safely invite two kids from his class or team and you're not compelled to invite the rest. Any more than that, and it's going to get nasty with mothers calling and asking why their darlings were excluded.

TIME IT RIGHT. Mornings are the ideal choice for party children and their guests who are under the age of four, since that's when they tend to be freshest and least meltdown prone. Eleven o'clock is generally the most manageable time—since it'll give you time to pull together last-minute party details and it will give us parents the chance to slap on some concealer and get ourselves out of the house. Even if this time slot clashes with some children's nap time, most can generally make it through an eleven o'clock party pretty well and nap afterward. The 11:00 A.M. party will also run into lunchtime and you will need to provide something for your young guests. But as you'll see when we talk about food—the amount will be minimal.

As far as slightly older children go, the time you choose will hinge around whether you want to serve a meal or not and what time your entertainment (if you're hiring any) is available. Some of the Girlfriends depend on the meal as just one more event to fill up the party schedule. We tend to stay away from serving dinner, however, unless the party theme itself focuses on food—like a taco- or pizza-making party. Then there are those of us who opt not to serve a meal at all, but prefer to simply keep the kids busy and stoke them with snacks. Prime start time for those parties (relieving you of the need to write "Meal Not Provided" on the invitation): anywhere between 1:30 and 3:30 P.M. Finally, you've got slumber parties—a subject we're not touching on too much since we think they're better for kids over the age of eight. But just in case you're wondering, the most strategic start time tends to be between 6 and 7 P.M. with a pizza thrown in for fuel—by the time kids are sleeping over, their parents are also pretty relaxed about nutrition.

CHOOSE THE RIGHT FINISH TIME. *It's whatever time is an hour and a half to two hours after your start time. Remember this and put it right on your invitation!!!* In general, the younger the birthday child, the shorter the bash should be. If the kids are old enough to be dropped off, try to greet each one and sweetly say, "Thanks for coming. See you at three, sharp!"

REMEMBER, BIRTHDAY PARTIES ARE A TWO-WAY STREET. Let's say after all this you still can't get the exact day and time you want or you absolutely must do it on a less than ideal date (like two days before Christmas). Don't panic. It doesn't mean disaster! Most of us parents will do our best to get our children to a party because we know—for the most part—they adore going. We also have crazy schedules ourselves and understand that's just how things must be sometimes. We only ask that you remember this when you get an inconvenient invitation and that you do your best not to get testy with us.

CHAPTER TEN

The Get-a-Grip Guest List

There's an old rule about how many guests to have at a child's birthday party. It goes something like "take your child's age and add one." Thus, if your child is turning five, for example, you should have six children at the party. That sounds just ducky but the Girlfriends can tell you flat out that this tactic doesn't generally cut it, as life is just not that tidy. Let's consider a birthday for that five-year-old child. If you're friendly with two neighboring families and each of them has two kids, that's more than half your guest list, never mind his two longtime pals from Gymboree, as well as his friends from school. And what if your child goes to a school that has an "all-or-nothing" rule about inviting classmates to birthday parties?

Even if you are able to trim the guest list, the Girlfriends warn against going too small. Experience has shown us that (a) it is rare that all invitees will be able to attend, and (b) of those who say they are coming, at least one or two of them will be a no-show due to an ear infection, bloody nose, or plain old bad mood. Our Girlfriend Beth hired a naturalist to come to her four-year-old's birthday and obeyed Woodsy Wendy's recommendation to have only ten children present. Well, Beth invited eight (figuring her twin birthday girls counted as two) and only four kids showed. Without a real "audience" Woodsy Wendy had few to participate in her routine, and without the buzz of a friendly crowd, the children got creeped out by the bugs and reptiles on display. Beth found herself scouring the neighborhood for siblings and footloose adolescents who were willing to fill the void. The twins had a good—if somewhat subdued—time all told, but Beth isn't too holy to admit that she was just a tad annoyed that she spent all that time and money putting together a party for a bunch of relative strangers.

Clearly, rigidity just doesn't work. The Girlfriends suggest you take the following approach instead:

First and Second Birthdays

As we've mentioned, we believe that first and second birthday *parties* are absolutely optional. If you do decide to throw a full-fledged fete for your child before she enters preschool, potential guests for your list will probably include:

Close relatives (if they live nearby)
Neighbors (if you're friendly)
Your best Girlfriends' children (if they spend time with your child)
Some family friends
A few miscellaneous "pals" your child has made on playdates (if he even has playdates)

Unless your extended family happens to be enormous, the Girl-friends have found it generally works out quite well early on if you put all of these players together. Yes, this can easily add up to a crowd of twenty or more. The upside here is that most of these folks will be grown-ups and loved ones who are truly looking for a way to help out. If you want to keep your workload down, throw the party on a weekday or Saturday morning and limit adult refreshments to coffee and pastries.

Third and Fourth Birthdays

Who you invite to your preschool-aged child's party largely depends on if she is—in fact—in preschool and how she feels about the kids in her class. If there's not a major connection there yet, the Girlfriends think you can get away with the guest list we've mentioned for the one- to two-year-old party and sim-ply bring cupcakes to school (as mentioned below). If your child does have a few buddies from class and the school doesn't have an all-or-nothing policy about party invitations, you can probably mix these kids in with the general masses without a problem. Should the school have an all-inclusive policy, however—and you and your child want to celebrate with classmates—you'll proba-bly want to do as we prescribe for parties for ages five to eight.

Fifth Through Eighth Birthdays

Matters get a big trickier when your little one enters grade school. Not only will she have particular ideas about who she wants at her party—she may very well tell you who she *doesn't* want there. For example, she may nix the very idea of inviting your best Girlfriend's daughter "who's not even in kindergarten yet (!)," and the "icky" boys next door (even though you go to their house for Thanksgiving every year). On the flip side, the party your child wants may not be tolerable for the guests you, the mommy, feel you "have" to invite. If your first-grade daughter really, really wants a princess tea party, will her three male cousins go AWOL? And will grandma really want to sit in a bowling alley for two hours while your first-grade group whoops it up?

At this point, the Girlfriends offer these three words of advice: Divide and conquer. Keep the major factions essentially separate and find a way for each one to celebrate with your child. *What? Are these girlfriends kidding???* That's probably what you're shrieking to yourself at this very moment, but hear us out.

Baseline Bashes

Celebration #1: The Celebration Fantastic

This party will be the big deal with the favors and written invitations and it will be limited to your child's actual peers. It's also known in the Great Children's Unconscious as the Day of a Million Gifts. How many children does one invite?

THERE'S THE ALL-CLASS OPTION. We have to admit that many of us have given in and had a big all-class bash at some point (and have survived to tell the tale). These events are definitely frenetic. They can be overwhelming. They are not for everyone, to say the least. They can also be pretty terrific since the kids know each other and are accustomed to playing together. Another plus: If your child doesn't have an obvious "set" of buddies (like if you've just moved into town or it's the very beginning of the school year), a party with his class can skirt the situation and help him get comfortable with the children he sees every day. Some hired help—even if it's simply a teenager from down the road—can make a big difference here.

THERE'S THE SINGLE-GENDER OPTION. Boys and girls naturally start snubbing each other somewhere between the age of five and eight. No matter how idealistic you might be, don't fight this development because it will (a) further convince your child how odious the opposite sex is—at least for now, and (b) help slim down the guest list dramatically. The single-gender option is an especially handy way to cut down on numbers if your child's school has an all-or-nothing policy about inviting classmates, since most schools won't argue the point if you make it clear that the event is boys or girls only.

THERE'S THE VERY-BEST-FRIENDS OPTION. As your child gets older and individual friendships get stronger, this concept will become more appealing. Encourage your child to invite two guests from class and one or two others from dance, soccer, or the neighborhood. Then Plan a party that makes the most of the group's small size. Our Girlfriend Heidi's two girls are allowed to have four guests max at their home parties. Heidi, in turn, is in the position to do all kinds of cool things with them. One year, the girls helped Heidi prepare an honest-to-goodness gourmet dinner, then dressed up in their finest clothes and ate their meal by candlelight. Our Girlfriend Liz has allowed her sons to invite four guests and their fathers to a professional hockey game. The party boys then came back to her house for cake and ice cream.

Celebration #2: Cupcakes at School

Up until about middle school, most teachers allow parents to come in and celebrate their child's birthday along with the class. No need to get fancy here. Make a batch of cupcakes from a mix and use prepared icing or just go out and buy some at the grocery store. Kids don't really care as long as the things have lots of frosting. Experienced Girlfriends urge you to skip the cute plastic decorations on top, since they are usually attached to very sharp toothpicks and instantly become weapons.

The Girlfriends heartily encourage you to do the cupcake thing for two reasons. First, in case you have forgotten, this is a pretty big deal for a child and really does make her feel special. If you don't do it, she may very well feel disappointed. Second, it will excuse your child (or you) if she's begged you for an all-class celebration outside of school but you just can't or don't want to pull off that feat. Lots of us Girlfriends with summer babies bring in cupcakes during the last month of school so our kids can celebrate with their classmates. Check with the teacher first— some prefer that mothers of summer babies coordinate and throw one big cupcake party for all of them on the same day.

Celebration #3: The "Real" Birthday

Chances are, your child's birthday party will not actually fall on her exact birthday. Even if this is, in fact, possible, the Girlfriends think it's something to at least consider avoiding. Here's why: A child's actual birthday is the perfect time to tie in with family, close neighbors, and other folks who don't—for one reason or another—make the list for the "friends" birthday party. On the minimalist side, simply extend an open invitation to all concerned to come and share some cake and blow out candles *after dinner.* Gifts from grandparents and mom and dad can be opened right then and there. (Believe us, they will get much more attention than if they are thrown in with the rest of the loot that comes with the "big" party. Opening gifts will also make the evening extra special.) Our Girlfriend Maria has a tradition where she tells the story of "What happened the day you were born," which her kids never tire of hearing. She times it to be about as long as it takes to eat a piece of cake. Your child gets her big day acknowledged and the relatives feel honored that they're the ones who were invited to share the occasion. If you feel you want to do something more, buy some balloons, order in some pizza or Chinese food, and have the gang for dinner. Remember though, there's no reason to get carried away with streamers and party favors. You are doing this already with the "kids' party."

By the way, all of this birthday nuttiness will calm down considerably as your child gets older. You will eventually be able to look a birthday straight in the face and know that it doesn't require confetti every time it's mentioned. Grandmas and grandpas may be less bent on being there on the big day—or they may not even be around at all anymore. Your child may shudder at the very idea of your showing up with cupcakes at school. Enjoy these days while they're here—like we mothers all tell you, they'll be gone before you know it.

CHAPTER ELEVEN

The Truth About Party Invitations

The Girlfriends are all for sending out cute party invitations; we just don't see any real value in spending too much time or money on them. Consider this scene (which is typical of most chaotic, child-inhabited households):

> *Mom collects the mail, rifles through it, and exclaims, "Oh Janey, there's a letter for you!" Four-year-old Janey is off in the playroom digging through the dress-up chest and can't be bothered to respond. Mom comes in, opens the envelope, and hands Janey an adorable hand-decorated ballerina slipper cut from cardboard and covered with pink felt (on the flip side, info about little Elaine Prescott's ballerina party is etched in metallic pink ink). Janey grasps the slipper, pets the felt for a few seconds, then puts it aside so she can pull on a pair of metallic-gold go-go boots. Mom picks up the abandoned invitation and quickly stashes it in her date book or on her desk, where six other party invites sit in a pile.*

Mom's date book, desk, or paper-cluttered refrigerator are really and truly where most birthday party invitations end up because we're the ones who must keep track of these events. Even if something particularly impressive arrives—like a plastic shovel for a backyard beach party or an actual pumpkin (which more than one Girlfriend child has received around Halloween), the impact isn't proportional to the money and energy that went into creating and delivering it. An awesome invitation has simply never determined whether our young kids attended a particular party or not. We personally have never sat up at night marveling at such things. We can also tell you that should children end up going to a particular party, they will still be expecting cool favors or neat prizes, regardless of how much the host mommy spent on the ingenious invitation she sent all those weeks (which might as well be years) ago.

The Girlfriends say keep those invitations simple. If you're pressed for time, pick up a few packs of party invitations that complement your theme (see Party Goods and Decorations for sources). If you are doing your party outside the home and the venue includes preprinted invites in its fee, we think it's nuts not to use them. If you do, however, want to do something a little creative, consider these strategies from some of the more evolved Girlfriends on the birthday party front:

PUT YOUR LITTLE ARTIST TO WORK. We love the idea of having kids make their own party invitations but think it's pretty impractical to expect a little person to decorate each and every one. (This scene usually winds up with mommy finishing off most of them at 1:00 A.M.) Instead—if your child is into the idea—encourage her to make one picture for the party on a standard white piece of 8½-by-11-inch paper. She might draw a fire engine for a fireman party, a doggy for a puppy party, or a pink teacup for a tea party. When she's done with the picture, mommy can draw some squiggles and doodads to sort of fill in the background if she wants. Next, fold the paper in half and write the party information inside (if your child is writing already, let her have a shot at this job). Now, tote that drawing to the local copy shop or office supply store and put the copy guy or gal to work making as many double-sided copies of your masterpiece as you'll need. Colored card stock is an option if you want to get fancy. All you'll need to do is fold them in half and stuff them into smallish manila or card-stock envelopes. By the way, if the drawing you want to use isn't on 8½-by-11-inch paper, have the copy gal shrink it down so it'll fit on a piece of paper that size, then write your party info inside. The point is that the invitation that ultimately gets copied must fit in a standard-size copy machine paper tray. Otherwise, things can get complicated and expensive. Of course, if you have a scanner connected to your computer at home, you can also scan the art and print out your own invites on regular paper or card stock.

DO THE PHOTO THING. If your babe is more inclined to eat a crayon than draw with it or if she simply doesn't want to create anything for the occasion, think about what you can do with photos. For her son's outer space party, our Girlfriend Catherine dug up a photo of Jake and glue sticked it onto a piece of paper. She cut out a cartoon drawing of a spaceship she found in some magazine and glued it onto the paper so it looked like Jake was standing on top of it. When Jake's collage work was color copied onto card stock at Staples, it really looked quite cute and campy. (All of this can, obviously, be done with computer clip art and a scanner if you're set up for it.) Then there's our Girlfriend Jill, who drums up parties for each of her four children with less effort than it takes most of us to make a weeknight dinner. She shoots a pic-

ture or two of her birthday child doing something goofy that
relates to the party theme—for her four-year-old son's LEGO
party she covered him completely with the colorful blocks except
for his face. She uses a digital camera, downloads the image to
her computer and prints individual invites out on her printer. If
you aren't digital, take photos with a plain old camera, create an
invitation around the print you like, then turn to that whiz at
your local copy shop and have him make color copies. (Again,
you could also scan the image into your computer.)

HIT THE INTERNET. Since young kids aren't necessarily checking their
e-mail on a regular basis and some moms don't have the chance
to get near a keyboard, the Girlfriends don't think sending e-vites
through cyberspace is an option at this point. What we do like,
however, are all those cool invites out there that you can down-
load free of charge and print out onto card stock or plain old
paper. If you are doing a character party (Arthur, SpongeBob
SquarePants) check the home website of the TV network affiliated with the show (www.nickjr.com, www.pbskids.org have
some goodies). Also use your search engine: Type in whatever
character or theme you're looking for, plus the word "invitations" (for example, your search entry would be: "scooby-doo" +
invitations, or "fire engine" + invitations). You'll be amazed at
what you come up with. FYI, Kinkos, Staples, and other commercial copiers are prohibited from reprinting almost every rec-
ognizable image from Mickey Mouse to The Rock because of
trademark laws, so if you use these pictures, you'll have to
reprint them yourself, and accept the risk that you might be vio-
lating somebody's copyrights and trademarks.

USE IMPRINTABLES. Lots of us Girlfriends take advantage of the
blank decorative card stock (also know as "imprintables") that's

now widely available at stationery and office supply stores. All we do is type the party info into a Word document, put that pretty paper in our printer tray, and hit print. No need to fill out individual invitations. And no technical wizardry necessary, we swear. An even easier option: Many of the better card shops and stationery stores now stock a huge array of fine imprintable papers (including cute kid-friendly patterns) **and they will print out the invites for you.** It'll cost you more than if you do the job yourself, but the cards look great and for some of us, the convenience is well worth it.

The Most Important Part of the Invitation . . . In-for-ma-tion

Now that you've got something cute to mail out (never hand them out in school; you avoid hurt feelings and lost invites) don't forget about the information that goes inside. Sounds obvious, but there's more to this than merely jotting down the date and start time. Namely:

PROVIDE AN "RSVP BY..." DATE. For some reason, as we mentioned before, RSVP'ing to birthday parties has become an optional concept, even if an RSVP is clearly written on the invitation. Providing an RSVP deadline won't necessarily make people more inclined to call, but it will give you unofficial license to chase them down for an answer. The RSVP date should be a week and a half to two weeks before the party, so you have time to get the appropriate amount of favors and party supplies.

INCLUDE A START TIME *AND* END TIME FOR THE PARTY. Parties usually unravel and get hairy when they've gone on too long. Make it perfectly clear when your little guests should arrive and when (ideally one and a half to two hours later) you will be turning them over to the local Y.

CLUE THEM IN ABOUT FOOD. If you'll be serving lunch to the kids, write "Lunch will be served." If you'll be putting out a spread for the grown-ups, too, you might write "Everyone is welcome to join us for lunch," or "Parents are welcome to join us for lunch."

GIVE A HEADS-UP ABOUT DRESS. Our Girlfriend Elaine put on a Powerpuff Girls party for her four-year-old daughter Rachael but forgot to mention that painting a huge Powerpuff Girls mural would be the main event. It's hard to tell who was more alarmed—Elaine, when fourteen little girls showed up in their best party dresses, or the moms, who came to pick up their paint-splattered darlings. Give parents warning on the invitation if things are going to get messy, if warm clothes will be needed for outside play, or if children should be bringing anything in particular (like a towel or swimsuit). Equally important, tell parents if a character, like Big Bird or a circus clown will be entertaining at the party. So many kids (and husbands) are terrified of people in costume that there's a phobia named for them, we just can't happen to remember what it is. We'll talk more about what you should and shouldn't expect guests to bring in a later chapter.

A Note About Thank-You Notes

While the Girlfriends unanimously believe that the art of writing thank-you notes ranks right up there with the ABCs when it comes to teaching our children important life skills, we are divided on whether early birthdays are the opportune time to start. Frankly some of us just can't see what a child learns when the mom is the one sitting down and writing twenty notes, pretending to be the birthday child, as in, "Dear Robbie, Thanks so much for the great kite. My mommy and I flew it today and it was fun." Certainly, it's nice for kids and their parents to get that little piece of mail acknowledging that their gift did not, in fact, disappear into the ether, but then again, there are some moms who pretty much expect any gift sent to a kid's party to vaporize.

There are others, among the Girlfriends, however, who toe the Emily Post line, even if it's not with engraved stationery. If you fall into the latter school and your child isn't old enough to write a note, there are many ways to involve her. You can buy the already printed, fill-in-the-blanks thank-you cards and let her write the giftor's name and her own, while you address and mention the gift (if you kept the cards with the gifts). Or simply allow her to help stuff the envelopes, put the stamps on, and toss the letters into the mailbox. Including a photo of each guest in their respective thank-you notes is a nice touch—and a great way to get rid of all those prints that don't quite make the photo album.

CHAPTER TWELVE

Partying at Home Plate

So you're thinking about staging this party yourself, huh? Terrific. The Girlfriends have lots of good advice to give. Before we get down to business, however, we want to make you aware that throwing the party yourself won't necessarily be cheaper than farming it out. Sometimes it surely can be. But in many cases, after all is said and done—between the food, and the activities, and the carpeting that must be replaced afterward (just kidding on that last one)—the "homespun" versus "hired out" cost advantage can end up being pretty much of a wash. Plain and simple, throw a home or home-style party because that's what you and your child want.

We also want you to know that the Girlfriends do not believe that the world is divided into "do-it-yourself party moms" and "rent-event party moms." We are equal opportunity revelers. The "right" birthday approach is basically what works for you (and your child) at any given time. One year you might choose to go all out, invite your child's entire class, organize the games yourself, and send them all home with themed, hand-decorated favors. We've all done the big bang at least once—and in many cases, followed up the next year with a quiet group trip to the movies. Some of us throw home parties for our summer babies, but do winter birthdays off premises since we simply don't have the space—or intestinal fortitude—to host hordes of guests inside our homes. (This especially applies to boys as they get older, bigger, and rowdier.) It's called balance. So before you go making any judgments about what other moms do for parties, consider the fact that over the years, exercising all the options may very well be your sanest choice.

The Girlfriends' Panic-Free Home Party Formula

Hosting a bunch of short, energetic individuals with limited attention spans and questionable judgment is a lot less daunting if you break down the party time block into manageable bites. This approach becomes particularly helpful once children reach the age of about four and are ready to truly play games and join in on activities. Here's how we approach the antics:

ASK A BEST FRIEND TO COME EARLY. Nobody, young or older, likes being the first guest. It usually takes three or four kids to make things rock and roll, so ask a comfortable buddy, baby-sitter, or other youngish person to come and help get the party revved up. As the kids get older and have more stamina, you can invite this buddy to stay after the party to help unwrap the gifts and break them in, too.

WELCOME GESTURE AND ICE BREAKER ACTIVITY (15 minutes). Ease start-of-the-party awkwardness by making kids and their parents feel like part of the action right away. As they arrive, you (or your birthday child, in an ideal world) might hand each guest a small Ziploc bag with a few crayons inside and direct them to a paper-covered table where they can do some coloring. If you're having a backyard luau, invite arriving guests to sit down around a big basket filled with paper flowers and stringing accessories so they can start making their own leis.

GROUP GET-TOGETHER (30 minutes). After most everyone arrives (this is always a judgment call by you and our advice is, "The sooner the better") you'll start the main party activities. For two- and three-year-olds, this can generally be a time for free play. As kids get older, you'll need more structure and more activities to keep their attention and prevent them from going wild. This might be when you start a few relay races or a big craft project. If entertainment is scheduled, you'll do it now.

SIDELINE ACTIVITIES. Put out a big bowl of Froot Loops and two-foot lengths of colored cord so kids can string their own necklaces. Set up a Girlfriend or teenage neighbor at a table and have her do some face painting or apply cool tattoos. Haul out some fun, easy-to-share toys and games you already have on hand (the sandbox, a play kitchen and plastic food). The idea here is to provide quiet alternate attractions for shyer children who don't want to be part of the main fray or a diversion to simply keep things humming when there's a lull in the action.

FOOD, CAKE, AND ICE CREAM (20 minutes). Round everyone up and bring on the chow (Veteran moms' tip: never serve scooped ice cream: Use bonbons or Dixie cups instead since they're a million times easier to dole out fast. Plus, they don't melt all over the cake, which some kids hate because they are generally against any one food type touching any other food type.)

CHILL TIME (15 minutes). As kids gradually peel away from the cake scene, have a quieter activity set up that any number of individuals can take part in. If you're hosting very young kids, have an animated grown-up start reading a story aloud.

SEND-OFF EVENT (10 minutes). Finish off the fete with something short, sweet, and exciting. Piñatas are always a huge hit (literally and figuratively) but this is a sensitive area for the Girlfriends. Yoda Vicki got to a point where she spirited her kids home early from any party once she spied a piñata waiting in the kitchen or already hanging from a tree. Call her crazy, but the concept of small, blindfolded people batting aimlessly with a stick so that they can scurry along the floor for fifty cents' worth of cheap candy suggests nothing but mayhem. Far more universally endorsed is to send the kids on a treasure hunt to find their favors. In a perfect world, parents will start packing up or showing up. Make sure everyone has all their favors and prizes and send them on their way. (Note about party favors—make them all the same and make five extras at least. It saves so much time not to be looking for little Daniel B.'s bag when you suspect Daniel S. already took it. The extras are for those pitiful faces on little brothers and sisters who come with mom for pickup and stand emptyhanded.)

By the way, you've probably noticed that we haven't factored opening gifts into the party formula. It's not a mistake. The Girlfriends are taking a stand here and saying that we think it's high time this clumsy tradition gets phased out. In fact, many Girlfriends have never even witnessed such a barbaric event since their own childhood. It's not just boring, but too envy-inspiring for kids to sit around and watch a birthday child open up one present after another—especially at large parties. It's also one more unnecessary opportunity for kids to feel one-upped or smugly superior, depending on what their parents can or choose to afford. We think thank-you notes are a much more graceful and discreet way for a gift giver's thought and effort to be acknowledged, especially as the kids get older and can actually write—and read.

How to Make This Home Party Perk—Our Top Tips

1. **Focus most of your time, energy, and money on what the kids are actually going to do and/or make at the party.** Everyone will tell you to plan a theme for your party and everyone isn't wrong. A theme gives a party some kind of focus, will get your birthday boy or girl extra psyched, and provides a creative "jumping off" point for you, the party maestro. Don't go overboard with the theme thing, however. One of the biggest boo-boos the Girlfriends made with our parties early on is that we got so carried away with the themed decorations, invitations, and menu, we neglected to focus on what really mattered. Our guests showed up and after one or two activities (that they went through far faster than anticipated), we didn't know what to do with all those little people.

2. **Avoid asking guests to do too much in the way of advance footwork.** It's a nice touch to have kids come in their jammies for a mock sleepover, but don't go overboard with your requests. Asking guests to come in costume or make something ahead of time can end up being a big burden on their good old mom, who probably has other kids and perhaps ten other birthdays to keep track of that month. If you do end up asking guests to bring something along (like a bathing suit or smock), be sure to have extra stuff on hand for children who arrive unprepared (probably because one of us mommies failed to read the entire invitation).

3. **Get lots of "big people" in on the action.** You would assume that the chief big person at this shindig (other than yourself) would be the father of your child, but you'd be wrong, for oh so many reasons: Either he's too busy shooting videos, snapshots, and digital images, or he's noticed a great football game on TV upstairs and has drifted away. The fact remains that young kids are far more likely to approach a set of swings, a coloring table, or a basket of beads if there's a friendly-looking grown-up there to make it look exciting and welcoming. And you, of course, can't be everywhere at once. If parents will be staying with their children at the party, put the more gregarious ones to work—chances are they'll jump at the chance to get busy and stop making small talk (why else do you think we're always clamoring to help clear cake plates?). Invite older cousins to come and lend a hand or hire a couple of teens from the neighborhood. Don't be afraid to invite well-behaved, slightly older chil-

dren to the party as well (such as a couple of an older siblings' friends). These guys can often help provide some direction and momentum to activities (like relay races) that may be a bit too challenging or complicated for little kids to carry on their own. Last but not least, free up yourself by doing as much advance work as possible. Your participation and interaction with the kids—and especially your birthday child—during the party will contribute immeasurably to the overall vibe.

4. **Set the mood with music.** Music will do more to get children (and their parents) in the spirit of things than practically any decoration you'll spend your money on. Put your husband or some bored-looking grown-up in charge of keeping the boom box busy and have him start about ten minutes before the first guest is expected. Use whatever CDs your child adores or pop in some lively grown-up tunes that are also kid friendly—Gipsy Kings comes to mind. If you want to go the extra distance—purchase or dig up a CD or two that compliments the theme. A universal Girlfriends' favorite is the Beach Boys' *Endless Summer* for backyard beach parties and the Beatles, since most of our kids already know "I Wanna Hold Your Hand"; the movie soundtrack from *Close Encounters of the Third Kind* for space parties; etc.

5. **Keep the party confined.** Keeping kids together will give the party a more cohesive feel and limit how much cleanup you'll have on your hands. Remember, a party at home is not a cooks' tour of your entire house. Define the party area indoors with pieces of furniture, gates if

you have them, and even streamers to help drive the point home. If nothing else works, ask your local fire department for a roll of that yellow "crime scene" tape and use it liberally. Otherwise, you'll find someone you vaguely know using your husband's electric shaver. Outdoors, if you don't have a gate that closes in your backyard, make it clear to guests and your parents where they are and aren't allowed to go. Show children which bathroom they are supposed to use and limit their indoor access to that very glamourous destination.

6. **Opt for activities that are just a little outrageous.** Lord knows you don't need to go to great expense to wow little people. Just think up wacky ways to bend everyday rules and rituals. Let them paint their feet and stomp all over a big piece of kraft paper. Invite a bunch of eight-year-old girls to wear their pj's to a daytime slumber party, pull all the shades down, and tell ghost stories. As part of a "gross out" party (perfect for seven-year-old boys), fill a soup pot with cold spaghetti and dare a bunch of blindfolded little daredevils to root through the "dead worms" for "rotten eyeballs" (peeled grapes). Then see who's brave enough to eat one (for a prize). This is the stuff that keeps children's attention and elicits squeals of delight, not to mention a great video opportunity.

7. **Put a Polaroid to work.** A Polaroid camera has got to be one of the best investments a party mom can make. Kids love the instant results and the prints can help tie together seemingly disparate party elements. For example, decorating picture frames may seem like an odd activity for a

"glamour girl" party. Snap photos of each girl when she's all dolled up, though, and voilà—you've got a great place to put the print and a perfect party favor. Better still, if you have a digital camera, you can snap away and have a helper pump out pictures on your printer.

8. **Give away lots of loot.** The Girlfriends have observed that kids are far more likely to play the games we've drummed up if a potential prize is involved in the equation. Scour the dollar store for all kinds of oddball stuff you can hand out. Or simply buy a bunch of gold foil–covered chocolate coins or tuck small bunches of red vine licorice into Baggies, or, here's a Sugar Buster idea, give away bottles of bubbles. At every opportunity, give something fun away to each and every child. If you're playing "pin the _____ on the _____," award the child who pins the object on the straightest or highest or who does it the fastest, etc. Since we all know life is never fair and some kids are better "players" than others, make sure that the party favor repeats many of the prizes so that everybody eventually shares in the booty.

9. **Anticipate the needs of your guests and their parents.** If you're putting on a party for very young children, set out sippy cups, masking tape and a Sharpie pen for parents who may have forgotten to bring their own. They will think you're the American Idol Mom and you'll help them keep track of their own darling's germs. If the party is outside, put out sunblocks, and—if water play is involved—even some extra swim diapers and towels. If the kids will be painting or getting dirty, pull

out big, old T-shirts and make them available as smocks. Provide adequate seating for parents who will be staying at the party—even a couple of throw pillows on the floor or a blanket in a shady spot on the lawn will make them feel welcome. Most important of all, *serve coffee and caffeinated soft drinks!* (Just keep them in the kitchen, away from where the little ones are selecting beverages, 'cause dollars to donuts, if they see a Coke, they're going for it.) Lots of moms, especially nursing ones, will appreciate gallons of bottled water, but most will need the Mommy Drug of Choice, caffeine, sooner or later.

10. **Plan for the weather.** If you're inviting more than just a few children, rain dates simply aren't a reasonable option here. Families are just too busy to keep two dates free and you'll end up pulling your own hair out trying to prepare for a virtually undeterminable number of guests. Watch the weather reports carefully if you're scheduling a party outside and have an alternative indoor plan—and some additional indoor activities—in mind should there be a monsoon over Miami forecast. (When it's merely sprinkling, many of us have still had the party outside and the kids didn't seem to give a hoot.) Most important, don't freak out. Make the most of the day you end up with and chances are your birthday child and her friends will follow suit.

11. **Go with the flow.** If your birthday child and her guests just can't get enough of your storytelling and beg you to read another book, go with it. If your guests are totally into decorating the picture frames you've set up as a craft,

don't rush them onto the next thing just because you have it scheduled. As long as they're having fun, you're in The Party Zone. Believe us—it'll be a lot easier to squeeze stuff in at the end of the party than it will be to fill up time should you break up something good for the sake of an activity that turns out to be a dud.

CHAPTER THIRTEEN

What You'll Need for a Home Party and Where to Find It

Theme Ideas

Chances are pretty darned good that—unless you and/or your child come up with some completely wacko concept—your party theme has been done and overdone by countless parents before you. And chances are oodles of these parents have blabbed about their big party ideas on the good ol' Internet. By all means, take advantage of their inventiveness and read what they have to say. Pluck up some concepts you like and use them if you like them. Do take a lot of this stuff with a grain of salt, however. Remember, a parent who's intense enough to enter her great party ideas on some Internet website is probably more intense about this stuff than you'll need or want to be. Along these lines, you might want to peruse some of the more commercial websites that drum up party ideas as part of their editorial fare. Again—keep in mind that these folks get paid to come up with new and nutsy party ideas on a constant basis. They don't necessarily put these parties on, nor do they face the time and budget constraints real moms do. Adopt ideas that make sense, and use good Girlfriend judgment (which we're sharing in this here book) to blow off what sounds unnecessary.

A few good websites to start with include:

- Birthday Party Ideas, www.birthdaypartyideas.com: More party ideas than you could ever want—submitted by parents from all over and listed categorically.

- Boardman's Birthday Party Ideas, www.boardmanweb.com: A family-run site featuring party theme ideas and party idea bulletin boards, plus links to party supply sources and the site for the Boardman family's rat-breeding business. Yes, you read it right.

- Epinions, www.epinions.com: This opinion site has a big birthday ideas section in its kids and family category.

- Family.com, www.family.com: It's worth checking out what this site has to say. Much of the content is based on content from the magazine *Family Fun*.

Party Goods and Decorations

Certainly, decorations help set the stage for a fun party. So buy lots of streamers and drape them all over the place. Pick up a heap of helium balloons and tie them up wherever you can or blow up your own and stick them up with tape. (Keep them out of young children's reach, though, since they can be a serious choking and suffocation hazard when popped.) Go ahead and buy some paper plates and cups (and, if you want, invitations) that match the theme. But forget all those fancy store-bought doodads and catchy table centerpieces that just sit there and look nice. We'll tell you flat out that kids hardly notice this stuff. Little people are dazzled by "decorations" they themselves can interact with. If you're having a "purple party" give the children their purple T-shirt favors at the start so they can wear them and essentially "decorate" the party with their own little bodies. When you have your guests paint or otherwise decorate a mural (our very favorite ice breaker activity) they make the main decoration right on the spot.

A money-saving tip: It's not the worst idea to buy tableware and accessories that match your theme, but you don't have to go the whole nine yards—from favor bags to forks—to achieve a nice effect. If you're having a Scooby-Doo party, for example, and the Scooby-Doo partyware is cute, but pricey—buy just a few key components, say the tablecloth, lunch plates, and cups. Then round out the settings with less expensive napkins, plastic ware, and cake plates that pick up one of the colors in the pattern. (Don't skimp by giving some kids plain plates and some kids patterned plates, however. You may wind up with a melee on your hands.) Remember, too, that this party is really for the kids—if you're serving food to grown-ups, none of us will cry if we don't get fancy cups and plates to match the theme.

Another thing: Don't waste money on party hats or blowers. First of all, the blowers are silent now, since it was discovered that the little whistle inside was a choking hazard, and the hats are just annoying. Second the Girlfriends can't tell you how many times we've shelled out for party blowers and hats—and completely forgotten to use them or failed to get the kids interested in the things. If you feel compelled to provide traditional party hats (for the five seconds they'll actually be used), do what our Girlfriend Jill does—keep the hats from your first party and just pull them out from storage year after year. The kids will never notice if they don't match the theme du jour. Same goes for store-bought birthday banners.

Shopping Sources

Where's a Girlfriend to get paper supplies and basic decorations? Here's our take on the party supply sources that are out there:

DISCOUNT PARTY STORES: For basic decoration materials and paper supplies, party supply superstores like the Party City and Smart and Final chains are probably your best option. They have a huge array of themed and nonthemed stuff and their prices are generally comparable with the discounted fare you'll find on the Internet. You also won't have to factor shipping time and costs into your plans. In most cases, you can make returns without a problem and—if your cousins from Canada announce they're coming at the last minute—you can always run out and pick up more supplies in the pattern/color you've already committed to.

ORIENTAL TRADING COMPANY (WWW.ORIENTAL.COM: 800-875-8480): The Girlfriends absolutely adore this ultra-inexpensive, occasionally silly catalogue/Internet source for "everything birthday." We'll be discussing it at length when we talk about favors. As far as paper goods go—the offerings here can be rather limited. If you aren't searching for a particular theme, however, or happen to come upon something you can live with—like a basic zoo design—by all means snatch it up. You'll end up spending about the same on an entire set of stuff for eight that you might for a mere stack of fancy cake plates elsewhere.

TOY SUPERSTORES AND GENERAL MERCHANDISERS: You can pretty much skip these. Compared to the party superstores, party supplies at places like Toys "Я" Us and Wal-Mart are pretty limited, as far as the Girlfriends' experience goes. If they do happen to have a pattern that you like, they may not have the components you want or enough of each to meet your needs.

CARD SHOPS AND STATIONERY STORES: Depending on the size of the store (and who's stocking it) you'll find a selection of party stuff ranging from hip to ho-hum. Whatever you encounter, it won't provide the best bang for your buck.

WHOLESALE CLUBS: Warehouse stores like Costco, BJ's, and SAM'S Club are a good place to pick up plain vanilla paper plates, plastic utensils, plastic cups, etc.—in army-size packages. Since the Girlfriends aren't encouraging you to invite a cast of thousands, buying your paper supplies at these places is a better option if you're stocking up for a summer full of barbecues.

PARTY SUPPLY INTERNET SITES: Key in "party supply"+"discount" on your search engine and you'll come up with a ton of sources. Most of these sites carry very similar stock—especially when it comes to licensed characters. Shop around though, because prices vary considerably. As far as cost goes, the lowest prices you'll find online often aren't any more competitive than what you'll come upon at a brick-and-mortar discounter like Party City—and remember, you'll have to pay shipping. Also beware—Internet retailers (not to be confused with established retailers that also happen to offer Internet shopping) can be fleeting and somewhat undependable. Our Girlfriend Mary Jane ordered online because it saved her a trip to the party supply store. Only half her order arrived in time for the big day, so she ended up running out anyway at the last minute. The rest of her Internet order never even arrived.

PARTY SUPPLY "PACKAGERS": Lots of people turn to catalogues like Birthday Express and companies like Birthday in a Box because they can theoretically buy everything they'll need for a themed party all in one package. The Girlfriends have gone this route and we generally haven't been very impressed. First of all, you'll be spending money on components we generally don't think are necessary—like that full array of patterned tableware and ditsy decorations. Second—packages are generally sold in sets of eight. Since most parties aren't that small (and you always need extras just to play it safe)—we've either had to buy another whole package or spend top dollar for à la carte settings. This really adds up. Third—while the display of stuff you're buying may look impressive in the catalogue or online, the array that arrives at your home generally seems sort of skimpy. Wouldn't ya know it—most of us have ended up fleshing out our supplies at the party store anyway.

Favors

The truth about favors is simple: Kids want candy.

No matter the ingenious ideas we parents come up with . . . no matter how much we spend . . . no matter how many zillion pounds of sugary treats are served at the party itself . . . kids still want to walk away with at least something that contributes to dental decay.

Why don't we Girlfriends simply recommend, then, that you stuff little bags with all kinds of chocolatey, chewy stuff and call favors a done deal? Because many parents won't particularly appreciate the gesture (to put it lightly). And, maybe, just maybe, there's something in us that wants to send our guests away with a favor that might be a tad useful or memorable.

Here are several ways various Girlfriends have found a happy middle ground—without spending a fortune.

THE GOOD GOODY BAG. Our big advice here is to focus more on the "bag" and less on the "goodies." Specifically, we mean that if you can come up with some kind of inexpensive container that's visually exciting and that can be used when it's emptied, most of your work is done. If you're having a firehouse party, for example, buy a bunch of plastic fire hats and write the name of a guest on each one. Hand them out at the beginning of the party so the kids can wear them around—then toss in a few sweet treats as they head out. If you're having a cowboy party, wrap up goodies in colorful bandanas and tie them with a piece of twine. If you can't find something that directly complements your party theme, choose something that complements the time of year—perhaps a plastic water bottle for summer or those plastic trick-or-treat pumpkins if the party is around Halloween time.

What should go inside? Skip traditional junky plastic favors all together, like plastic gem rings, mini yo-yos, get the ball in the man's ears puzzles, and beaded necklaces. (The only exception in households with boys, in particular, have been the tiny parachuters they can throw off a balcony or from the top of some stairs.) Every mom in America can attest to the fact that this stuff generally ends up broken, under the sofa, or in the garbage within hours after a party ends. Since the "real" gift is the container itself, you can get away with tossing in a few pieces of candy, some stickers, tattoos, and perhaps a cool pencil. If the container is roomy enough, kids can fill it up with the other great loot they'll collect during the party. If, perchance, you want to put fancier stuff in the goody container, buy bulk packs of markers, crayons, Matchbox cars, lunch-size snacks (like Fruit Roll-Ups, Ritz Bits, chewy granola bars, etc.)—and divide up that stuff among the bags.

THE ONE-HIT WONDER. It's possible to send kids home with one single splashy favor without spending an arm and a leg or making the actual birthday presents look pathetic. It's all in the presentation. If you're having a backyard beach party for your preschooler, order a batch of beach balls in bulk. Don't hand them out when they're flat and all folded up, though. Blow them up yourself before the guests arrive, write a child's name on each one, then let them play with and bring their prize home. For a luau, order a bunch of dirt-cheap "luau" kits (complete with raffia hula skirts, leis, and bracelets), take them out of their yucky shrink wrap and present them to each guest as they arrive so they can wear their favor and liven up the party. If you're having a mock sleepover or a detective party, pick up a bunch of cheap flashlights (plus batteries to fill them) and personalize them with each child's name. Or how about a storybook or small journal for each child? For a little girl's tea party, send each guest home with a Chinese paper parasol—they're big, they're exotic, and they cost almost nothing (see Oriental Trading Company for this one). Take it from the Girlfriends that regardless of what you give, the kids will still expect candy. So find a way to incorporate candy into the party some other way—make it part of the treasure hunt or finish off the affair with a piñata. Let them take the sweet stuff home in a paper lunch bag or plastic bag. Or tie tissue paper bundles of treats to the strings of helium balloons, bring them out at the end of the party and hand one to each guest—they'll love it.

THE MAKE-IT-YOURSELF FAVOR. In case you haven't noticed, the Girlfriends have a strong affection for party paraphernalia that can do double or even triple duty. Nowhere else is the opportunity greater than with the "make-it-yourself favor." Not only do they relieve you from making and prepping party favors yourself, they keep your guests busy, they add to the scenery, and they make a memorable take-home gift. For this reason, the Girl-friends are often willing to spend some money on materials in this department. A good example: for a springtime party, have guests decorate their own terra-cotta pot with fast-drying fabric paint markers. After the birthday cake, let them each pick out a flower from a bunch of flats you've picked up at a plant nursery. Then help the kids pot their own plants (ask the nursery for potting tips and materials). See our section on Main Event Crafts and Activities on page 174 for more ideas and where you can get details about actually tackling these activities.

Where to Buy Favor Supplies

Think out of the box about where to get all this prize and favor stuff. Here are some good bets:

ORIENTAL TRADING COMPANY: We're not so hot on all the inexpensive favors this company offers, but we adore a lot of the other stuff—it just takes some digging to locate the "real-finds." Oriental Trading has got tons of potential goody holders, from plastic pencil cases and smiley face mugs to shiny, colorful Chinese take-out style boxes. Oriental Trading is also a super inexpensive source for candy, stickers, tattoos, kooky sunglasses, girly nail polish and hair stuff, anything luau and beach balls.

THE HOME DEPOT AND OTHER HOME SUPPLY SUPERSTORES: Don't let those burly plumbing contractors, no-frills displays, and loud chain saws fool you. These places are gold mines for moms in search of party stuff. It just takes a little imagination and some chutzpah to ask for help. As we mentioned, these are the places to pick up giant plywood boards for mural making (as well as makeshift tables). Load up on squares of ceramic tile for next to nothing and let each party child paint her own trivet. The brightly colored buckets in the paint section are easy to personalize or decorate with permanent markers. You may even be able pick up child-size Home Depot utility aprons.

HOBBY AND CRAFT STORES: Stores like A.C. Moore, Michael's, and the Rag Shop are brimming with all kinds of possibilities. It's here that you can pick up inexpensive beads and all the stringing accessories you'll need to go with them. This is where you'll find canvas tote bags, aprons, visors, and other "paint-your-own goodies" like light switch plates and unpainted wooden boxes. Even more important, you can usually scare up a salesperson— or crafty fellow shopper—who can show you exactly what paints, brushes, gadgets, and know-how you'll need to take on the project.

WAREHOUSE STORES: These are great places to buy snack foods, novelty candies (like fancy designer lollipops), candies, and art supplies like glue sticks, crayons, and markers in bulk. Also check out the book section to see what you might be able to pick up— these make good single favors. If you're providing food for a gang—including the parents—you might want to buy your eats here, as well. Ready-made crudités platters, shrimp rings, and all manner of baked goods abound. And many folks swear by their jumbo sheet cakes.

DOLLAR STORES: If you have one of these near your home—or something of the same ilk, like an Odd Lot, Family Dollar, or Job Lot—by all means stop by. They are the perfect source for random prizes you might want to give away during the course of the party. You might also find stuff for party favors here.

THE GOOD OL' INTERNET: You never know what you might come up with. Plug in "children's aprons" and you might very well pinpoint a source that sells 'em cheap and in fifteen different colors. Plug in "children's party favors" and you might find a source that personalizes all kinds of stuff on the cheap. We're not mentioning specifics here because, knowing the Internet, they'll vaporize by the time this book comes out.

Forget the Food, Where's the Cake?

Party after party, the Girlfriends have watched entire plates of untouched food get tossed into the trash. This includes tiny little turkey sandwiches with the crusts thoughtfully trimmed off. We've watched carrots cut to look like flowers wilt away on the tray and mini swimming pools made of blue Jell-O melt into a molten mess.

Save yourself the headache and expense. Stop the obscene amount of waste. Don't spend too much money or too much time on food that may very well go untouched. When you're dealing with young kids especially, the only edible interest they have is in the sweet stuff that comes out with the candles. The Girlfriends have finally accepted this fact and have resigned ourselves to keeping everything that comes before the cake and ice cream pretty darned prosaic.

For Children Four and Under

These kids aren't generally adventurous eaters and a birthday party probably isn't the place they're going to change their ways. Think in terms of simple, familiar foods that won't make anyone choke (or gag). The Girlfriends' suggestions:

SNACKS: Shallow trays filled with dry treats like pretzels, goldfish, and cheese puffs (avoid popcorn, tortilla chips and any small, round, hard, or crumbly treats that can pose a choking hazard).

DRINKS: Apple juice, orange juice, and lemonade. Although no juice box in the history of peewee birthday parties has ever been finished, lots of Girlfriends are willing to suck up the marginal expense and waste of sugar water and stick to Capri-Suns or drinks in small-size boxes that don't spill too easily. You may also want to fill a basket with preassembled sippy cups, masking tape, and Sharpies for identification.

LUNCH: Forget the grill—lots of kids hate the "black stuff" it leaves on the food. Besides, having a big, hot thing going during a children's party adds an extra edge you don't need and can unnecessarily sidetrack dad. You're better off with:

> **Pizza** cut into half slices.
>
> **Chicken nuggets/fingers:** Buy them in bulk at the warehouse club, heat them on a cookie sheet in the oven, toss into a cloth-lined basket.
>
> **A large batch of macaroni and cheese**—from a mix is perfectly acceptable.
>
> **Cucumber sticks and cut-up fresh fruit,** if it will make you feel good. Carrots would seem like natural additions here, but we're still concerned with the choking thing.

For Children Five to Eight

Napping isn't an issue with these seasoned partiers, so it's easier to schedule a party in the afternoon and thus possibly avoid serving lunch. If you do choose to serve a meal—and in some locales it's practically a given—the food can be a little more interesting or clever and you don't have to worry so much about choke foods, unless younger siblings will be present.

SNACKS: If no little chokers will be present, add tortilla chips to the mix if you want, as well as grapes, baby carrots, and other finger foods.

DRINKS: Kids this age probably want soda—God knows how their parents feel. Tread a safe path and put out foil sacks of fruit-ades and sports drinks. To minimize stain damage, stay away from all those red and purple drinks.

LUNCH: If you want to keep things easy, go for the same menu options we've recommended for the younger kids. Pizza's a standard for a reason: It's easy, kids love it, and it's delivered right to your door. Children at this point also love putting together their own creations and concoctions so you might want to make the meal more interactive. On the simple side, create a fixin's bar for the chicken nuggets (think in terms of bottled honey mustard dressing, barbecue sauce, sweet and sour sauce, ketchup, etc.). Buy a bunch of prepared mini pizza crusts, let the kids add their own toppings, and pop them into the oven. You can set up a taco bar, or even a build-your-own sandwich bar with an array of sliced cheese, meats, condiments, and chips. By making the meal prep an activity, you have yet another opportunity to make a party element do double duty.

Feeding the Big Mouths

When children are still young enough to need a parent with them at a party, the Girlfriends think it's a gracious gesture to provide some eats beyond chicken nuggets and Goldfish. If it's a morning party, you might provide:

"Leaded and unleaded" coffee and tea
Bottled water (both cold and room temperature)
Iced tea
Mini muffins
Bagels and cream cheese
Cut-up fresh fruit
Raw baby carrots

If you end up throwing a family and friends party and intend to serve everyone lunch, keep these tips and ideas in mind:

- Don't serve anything that requires last-minute preparation.

- Forget the grill. Yes, it's an irresistible idea if you're doing a backyard bash, but as we've said, it can be dangerous and it ties up dad.

- Think salads. They really do solve lots of problems since they don't need to be heated, they don't generally require a knife (handy, since parents often end up eating while they're standing up or with their plate on their laps), and most of the prep can be done a day ahead. If the salads aren't too exotic, children who don't want the same old kid stuff can get in on the grown up fare. Add some fresh crusty bread and slice fresh fruit and veggies (or just a heap of grapes and bowl of baby carrots if you want to minimize chopping work) and you'll be in great shape.

The Cake

Some Girlfriends make their own cakes, God bless them. Some of us order them. We all agree that the birthday cake is a big deal. This is, after all, what kids associate with birthday parties and it's what they look forward to.

From the bake-it-ourselves contingent, here are our top tips:

DON'T GET BOGGED DOWN BY COMPLICATED DESIGNS. Sites like www.family.com offer all kinds of way-out and wonderful cake concepts. Use them as inspiration but don't feel bound to everything they say. If a concept calls for six different kinds of candy—and you don't feel like buying each and every one—be creative and make do with what you have. For example, could a red Fruit Roll-Up from your pantry do the same job as a flattened red gumdrop? Can a raisin take the place of an M&M?

SHEET CAKES ARE THE WAY TO GO. Slices from a classic, layered cake are too big for small children and don't provide as many portions. Layer cakes also don't provide the surface space you'll need to have fun with the decorations.

DON'T DO ANYTHING FROM SCRATCH. Children can't tell the difference between a batter that comes from a box and the one you whip up from your grandma's recipe file. Experience tells us that the real energy should be spent on decorating the cake.

BAKE MORE CAKE THAN YOU MAY ACTUALLY NEED. If you're doing anything the least bit creative with the shape of a cake, the job will be less stressful if you have lots of "construction" material to work with. It's also helpful to have extra frosting on hand—the Girlfriends can't count how many times we've run out with only half the cake covered. It also makes good "mortar" for patching up mistakes.

USE CARDBOARD AS YOUR CAKE PLATTER. Cut a big, flat piece of thick cardboard from one of those boxes in your recycling pile. Cover it with aluminum foil and tape the edges of the foil to the underside. Then, set your cake down on that. It makes a splashy presentation and leaves lots of room for adding colorful decorations around the cake itself.

TURN CAKE TIME INTO AN ACTIVITY. Make cupcakes instead and have the kids decorate their own.

Some tips from the bakery cake contingent:

CONSIDER ORDERING FROM A WAREHOUSE CLUB. The cakes are big, delicious, and the price can't be beat.

IF YOU DON'T SEE A DESIGN YOU LIKE IN THE BAKERY'S CAKE BOOK, ASK. Lots of us have been surprised by how willing these folks are to take a stab at a new idea. Bring them a sample party plate to copy the main character.

IF YOU WANT TO KILL TWO BIRDS WITH ONE STONE, SERVE ICE CREAM CAKE. Remember, though, to take it out well in advance so you don't wind up attacking the thing with a sledgehammer.

Outside Entertainment and Hired Helpers

The Girlfriends can tell you right now that a lot of what makes a children's party exciting and fun is the charisma and creativity of the parents who are throwing the party. Our Girlfriend Felicia, for example, relishes the whole idea of running around with the kids and can turn just about any activity—even if it's throwing juice boxes in the trash—into a wild and wacky event. (She's also the type who makes friends while waiting in line at the Division of Motor Vehicles.)

For many of us Girlfriends, however, the prospect of entertaining a bunch of kids for an extended period of time (especially while other parents look on) makes a root canal seem like a cake walk. It's not the work, mind you. We're just not natural-born Pied Pipers and couldn't learn to be even if we tried. If you fall into this category, consider doing what we do: Get help. Not the Freud variety, thank you very much. We're talking about hiring someone or something to drum up some fun and add structure to the party. This takes a lot of pressure off good old mom, since it generally takes care of that "main activity" part of the event. With a low-key ice breaker activity to start and a piñata or treasure hunt to finish off, you've got a nice, neat party. In general, you don't even need to provide a full meal unless that happens to be something you have your heart set on doing.

The Usual Suspects

They may be corny, they may be cliché, but party staples like puppeteers, clowns, and magicians really do delight children. Why else do you think these guys are still doing the rounds with their skinny balloons after all these decades? Heck, some of us

Girlfriends have hired those "party planners" to come to our homes and handle everything and it wasn't bad at all (except for the fact that it often cost us a bundle). These days, you can also find new and offbeat twists among the party people ranks—there are reptile folks who will bring their scaly friends to your home; naturalists who will lead nature walks in your backyard; there are mad science guys who will conduct all kinds of crazy experiments; there are chefs who will cook up a storm with the kids. Our big word of caution about all professional party entertainers—just like every other party pundit's—is: See these folks in action—or at least meet the individuals—before you take them on. Failing that, get the names of some referrals and grill these moms for details. Did Mimi Macaroni show up on time? What did she do that the kids liked? Was there anything they didn't really dig? Did Mimi seem open to working with you? Did she make an effort to personalize her show? Did she reach out to the birthday girl and make her feel special? Did Ms. Macaroni seem like she was happy to be there? Was she in a rush to leave? Did she bring any interesting props, activities, or giveaways with her? Did she seem sober (that one is from our friend Helen)? Did she have B.O.? (Kids like that even less than us grown-ups.)

You can usually figure out what's available near you by checking the local papers or activity guides and asking around at school. You might also check www.birthdaypartydirectory.com to see what specialty acts they list in your area.

Jump for fun!

We just can't write about birthday parties without touching on those ubiquitous inflatable moon bounces that come shaped liked castles, dinosaurs, and even Woody from Toy Story. For every child who shyly aims for the sideline activities will be two who have more combustive energy than a steam locomotive. These things just can't help but scream "Birthday!" and kids love them. You can hire them for under $100 in some areas, if you take the responsibility of placing one or two adult monitors to remind the jumpers to take their shoes off and enforce rules like "No ninja jumps or wrestling holds." If you would rather hire that job out with the rental, chances are it will cost closer to $300 and that pretty much eats up your entertainment budget, but millions of enthusiastic moms and dads call it money well spent. We have a Los Angeles friend who has two toddlers and his brother and sister-in-law were coming for a visit with their preschoolers. He called his connection for the $75 moon bounce and the parents took turns being the one on duty while the others sunbathed and had cocktails. He couldn't have gotten a sitter for less if he'd wanted.

Other Ideas

What the Girlfriends would like to do now is get you thinking about some of the less obvious—and often less expensive—options out there.

Recruit "Experts" You and Your Child Already Know

We adults might think it's nice to have someone fresh, new, and surprising appear at the birthday parties we throw. Kids, however, often feel otherwise. (The Girlfriends are sure you've been to at least one soiree where a giant purple dinosaur danced into the living room and scared the bejeezus out of half his young audience.) What makes children feel special, important—and comfortable—in many cases, is having a grown-up they like and admire come to share their big day, give them lots of attention, and meet their friends. If there's no one like this in your child's life (save the man who drives the ice-cream truck) think of an "expert" you know personally and think your child might like. Some of the folks the Girlfriends have informally hired include:

Hairdressers: If the gal who cuts your daughter's hair is a charmer, ask her if she'd be up for a little freelance work doing a beauty birthday at your home. Our Girlfriend Tanya paid the stylist at her local Supercuts about $150, then stocked up on all kinds of fun stuff for Caroline and the girls to have fun with—nail polish in every color, hair scrunchies, clips, temporary hair tints, etc. With bubblegum pop playing in the background and lots of snacks to keep them stoked, the girls worked on each other's makeup, then moved on so Caroline could "do" their do's. They were each sent home with lots of Polaroids and a handful of fun hair accessories they picked out during the party. Along the same lines: If you spend a lot of time up close and personal with cosmetic counter ladies at your local department store, see if one of them will make an appearance at your party. Our Girlfriend Amanda did this (we won't mention the brand since we don't want to incriminate anyone) and the gal showed up with two suitcases filled with samples. (Amanda herself is still using the stuff to this day.)

Coaches: If your son or daughter plays on a soccer or T-ball team or if they take lessons, see if one of the instructors might lead a mini clinic in your backyard. If you don't have space, you may be able to reserve one of the playing fields in your town—it'll cost you little if anything.

Class Instructors: Think about the classes your child has taken and what she's enjoyed. Chances are that many of those instructors and group leaders would be happy to earn some extra bucks. Among the individuals we've hired for our home parties: Story-time people from the local library or bookstore; instructors from Mommy and Me music classes; student teachers from school—especially from art and gym class. There are lots of options here, just keep in mind that whatever activity you choose should be enjoyable for children even if they don't have the level of experience or skill your child does. (Our Girlfriend Jenny attended a tae kwon do party where no one could keep up with the leader. It ended up being a one-man performance for the birthday boy and a big bore for everyone else.) In many cases, making a particular discipline accessible to a diverse group has to do with how party "classes" are taught—so have a discussion with the instructor about how this might be done before you hire him or her on.

Carpenters and other handymen and -women: If you and your husband are hopeless around the house, chances are you already know a handyman or carpenter better than you'd like to (not to mention your plumber and electrician, but these guys aren't so great for parties, considering their specialty). If this individual is an affable sort, see if he'll pitch in at your child's party. Our Girlfriend Jill paid her carpenter to help her out and it was a booming success: She purchased a bunch of inexpensive tools and hardware that Jim recommended and cleaned out her basement so there was plenty of work space. On the day of the party, Jim showed up with kits of precut wood and helped each little guest build his own bird house. Jim wasn't as lively as a hired clown (he was, in fact, slightly reminiscent of Oscar Madison), but he was very helpful with the children. All Jill and her husband had to do was keep things fun and lively and hand out snacks.

Track Down Teenagers and College Students: There's almost nothing more exciting for a young child than the attention of a teenager. We moms get pretty darned excited about teens and college students ourselves, since they're such a great source of inexpensive—and potentially enthusiastic—help. If you have a charismatic high schooler who baby-sits for you, have her enlist some friends. Ask nice teens in the neighborhood or enlist the help of older cousins. For the price of one professional hairstylist, our Girlfriend Bonnie hired five teens from her apartment building to come and set up "shop" in her living room for her eight-year-old's glamour girl party. One manned a makeup table, another took care of manicures, another painted toenails, two worked on hair. The little girls were thrilled to pieces to be the focus of attention. For the big girls, the chance to play with all of the stuff and attend the party was almost more exciting than the money they received for their help. If you can't afford a soccer coach, hire a couple of teens who play on the high school soccer team and let them get out and play with the kids and—in an ideal world—dad or mom. If you simply need extra hands or extra energy at your party, teens are also the ones to turn to. Remember—these kids aren't going to run activities and direct events like the pros will. You'll need to take on that job and use them as your foot soldiers. Also make sure that the teens you hire won't be "too cool" to let loose and have fun with the children.

CHAPTER FOURTEEN

What Are These Kids Going to Do?

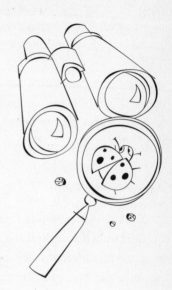

Six Easy Arrival Activities

When children start trickling in, have an activity they can get busy with right away. Here, some very simple ideas:

Ages Three to Five

BUBBLES: Hand each child a bubble wand when they arrive, then point them in the direction of a shallow pan filled with bubble liquid. If the babes are young, their parents will help them blow. Individual bottles of bubbles work, too.

DECORATE THE TABLECLOTH: Instead of purchasing a traditional paper tablecloth, tape a long stretch of butcher or kraft paper down the length of the table. Place several plastic containers (or creative "holders" to match your theme, such as toy trucks or overturned fire hats) along the table and fill them with markers, crayons, and glitter pens. Let the children decorate the paper—then use it as the tablecloth when lunch and cake are served.

DECORATE-YOUR-OWN PARTY CROWN: Cut shapes out from craft foam yourself or buy precut gold crowns from a hobby or party store. Put out glitter pens, glue sticks, stickers, plastic gems, and feathers.

Ages Five to Eight

DECORATE-YOUR-OWN FAVOR BUCKET: When children arrive, hand them a plastic sand bucket and send them off to decorate it with lots of stickers and different color permanent ink markers. The kids can then use the bucket to hold the goodies they collect during the party.

JELLY BEAN GUESS: Fill a jar with jelly beans, M&Ms, or some other type of small treat—count how much there are in advance. If you want, try to match the party theme—you might use chocolate balls covered with ladybug patterned foil or baseball-patterned foil, for example. Put out pencils and small slips of paper. Ask kids to guess how many goodies are in the jar, help them write it down on the paper with their name, and drop the paper into a shoe box with a slit on top. At the end of the party, gather the kids around and award the treat jar to the child whose guess was the closest.

COOPERATIVE BIRTHDAY MURAL: This one isn't quite as simple as the others, but it's a great way to start out a party and kids will keep coming back to it.

Basic Materials:

- For an indoor party, use a long stretch of **mural-sized kraft or butcher paper** (see page **30** for sources and the Girl-friends' reasons for keeping this stuff on hand all the time). For minimal mess, set up a few low tables with **crayons, washable markers, glitter glue, and stickers** for the kids to use.

- For an outdoor party, use heavy craft paper and tape it to a fence, if you have one. Alternatively, pick up the cheapest biggest **piece of plywood** you can find in the lumber section at The Home Depot (it should cost you between eight and twenty dollars). If the thing doesn't fit in the back of your minivan or station wagon, the guys will usually tie it to the roof of your car free of charge. Use a **roller to paint the board with white primer or any old white paint that's cheap.** Set out tempera paints on low tables and let the kids go nuts. If you take the plywood approach, you can wash the paint off pretty well with a garden hose when the canvas gets full and let the kids go at it again. If you repaint the board white, you can reuse it for years to come.

ADAPTOMATIC: Use permanent black marker (like a Sharpie) to write out a message in bubble letters and draw basic forms the kids can then color in. For example, if the party has a "sports theme" you might write "Happy Birthday William! Let's Have a Ball!" at the top, then draw basic outlines of basketballs, foot-balls, baseballs, etc. For a garden party, spell out "Happy Birth-day" and "Here's to Our Growing Girl!" then draw all kinds of simple flowers and leaves, small and large, for the kids to color in. For an underwater party, draw some basic fish, starfish, seaweed, coral, and rocks. If you have no artistic ability whatsoever, write the names of the party guests in bubble letters all over the canvas and let them color in the letters and decorate them (with their parent's help, if necessary).

Main Event Crafts and Activities

Fact: Any activity you plan for a birthday party will take about one-eighth of the amount of time you expect it to. This may not sound startling or upsetting to you in abstract—but when you find yourself ten minutes into your child's party and you've exhausted all your planned events, the next eighty minutes can begin to feel like the longest and slowest in your life (second only to the ones you wait out while Ferberizing your baby). It can also be sort of distressing if you've spent three hours putting together the props for an activity, only to see it over in a flash or passed up by the kids altogether.

Our advice is to have a couple of "big activities" in mind (that don't require a heap of advance prep), plus a handful of simple "off the cuff" ideas in the hopper. If the kids end up having a blast all on their own after the main events are out of the way, go with the flow. If there's a twiddle-your-thumbs lull, you'll know what to do.

One more caveat: While you're drumming up activity and craft ideas, really take your party children's age into consideration. This isn't the time to overreach because you think your particular offspring is a genius or that kids these days aren't challenged enough. The Girlfriends can tell you that a party vibe is the best when all the children understand what's happening and feel confident enough to participate.

Where to Get Activity Ideas

For an exhaustive list of classic party games and a refresher on how to actually play them, log onto www.gameskidsplay.com. You can also simply plug "party games" or "party activities" into your search engine and score a nice array of sources. Check in, too, with your child's class or gym teacher at school. With all the time these pros spend on the playground and in the classroom, they're sure to have the inside skinny on what the kids are up to and into.

If you want ideas about simple crafts, you'll find about a bazillion sources on the Internet and umpteen books on the subject. If all this overwhelms you, we have a simple suggestion: Report to your local hobby store, find one of the folks who works in the children's craft section or who runs the children's crafts sessions, and see what they suggest. Also check out our Easy Projects for the Artistically Challenged section in Chapter Two.

Here's the Girlfriends' short list of sure-bet party activities and craft ideas:

TREASURE HUNTS. Kids absolutely adore treasure hunts—when they're done right. The key is to (a) make it age appropriate, (b) keep it simple, and (c) make sure that there's a payoff the kids will appreciate. Girlfriend moms love treasure hunts because they can be done outdoors nearly year-round and—in the case of torrential rain—can be staged in a playroom at the eleventh hour.

For kids between three and four, do treasure hunts much like you do Easter egg hunts. Hide lots of stuff that's instantly interesting and rewarding (candy that's not a choke hazard, stickers, tattoos), arm the kids with cute containers or bags, and send them out to round up the loot. This is the perfect send-off at the end of a party because whatever the children collect becomes the favors they take home.

For children five to eight, you can (but don't need to) add an extra step to make it more interesting. Our Girlfriend Cathy hid foil-covered chocolate coins around her yard. (You can really use anything that's cheap, easy to spot, and abundant—packing peanuts will do the trick.) The kids were sent out to find them, with a limit of fifteen each, and then "redeemed" their coins for goodies set out on a big picnic table (a jump rope was worth two peanuts, a pretty barrette was worth five, an old Happy Meal toy was worth one, etc.). You can hide something as simple as real peanuts and reward the kids with one tattoo for every five or ten they find. Traditional treasure hunts—where one clue leads to another and ultimately to a box full of loot—like party favors—can work. If you put your effort into one of these, save it for a small group of kids no younger than six.

Adaptomatic: If you want to do a treasure hunt at the start of your party, have the kids hunt for items they'll need for the next activity. Hide the sea sponges and cut-up kitchen sponges you'll be using to sponge paint. If you're having a luau, tuck away the flowers the girls will use for stringing leis. Set a limit and tell kids that when they reach it, they can help other children hunt down their treasure.

PIN THE WHATEVER ON THE WHATEVER. Most of us moms love this party staple because there's not a theme in the world to which it can't be adapted. Kids run hot or cold on the game—depending on how it's done and the mood of the party at the moment. That's why we advise you not to personally pour too much time into preparing the props yourself. The ideal tactic is let the kids make the things they'll be "pinning"; it'll give the party some continuity and the kids will take some pride in the playing pieces they've made.

Children three to four: In our experience, little people do not dig the idea of being blindfolded. Don't push it if they don't want to. Devote most of the time to decorating the playing pieces with the children (make basic cardboard or craft foam cutouts ahead of time and write one name on each with permanent ink pen). Attach double-sided tape to each. Then have them simply take turns attaching their art to a board with a number of interesting targets drawn on it. Should they want to try the game blindfolded, simply specify which target on the board they should aim for. For example, for a space party our Girlfriend Pam covered a big piece of cardboard with shiny black paint. She then used tempera paints to draw bright colored planets all over it. The children each had their chance to stick the "space shuttle" they had decorated wherever they pleased on the board—on a planet, in space, etc. The board made a wonderful decoration for the party and at the end of all the excitement, the children got to remove their space shuttles from the board and take them home. The only outstanding issue is whether to allow your birthday boy/girl to go first. We say "yes" until about the age of five, when they will have learned something about being a good host/hostess and sharing with friends.

Children five to eight: Have the kids make their playing pieces, then play the game with blindfolds on. The older the child, the more you should spin her or him. Announce from the get-go that you'll be awarding prizes—and do so for all kinds of crazy reasons and accomplishments. The "Wiggliest Walker," the "Most Off Target," etc. If you're dealing with eight-year-olds, you might have to make the game even cooler. Use a poster of a celeb, like Britney Spears, for example. Then play "pin the sunglasses, miniskirt" on Britney.

Adaptomatic: We've seen and done everything from Pin the Wart on the Witch's Nose to Pin the Alien on the Spaceship to Pin the Boobs on Pamela Anderson (okay, that was a grown-up party).

FISHING FOR FAVORS. Make a crude fishing rod by tying a length of cord to the end of a sturdy stick (try unscrewing the "broom" off the bottom of a broomstick—if you're really in luck, the top of the broomstick will have a hole onto which you can tie cord). Tie a clothespin onto the other end of the cord. Give a parent or helpful teenager a box filled with an array of goodies and station him behind a barrier of some kind so the children can't see what he's up to. He might hide behind a sofa that you've covered with a sheet or two. You can also tie a cord about four or five feet off the ground across a corner of a room, drape a sheet over the cord and have the grown-up hide in the corner behind it. Let the children take turns clipping a gummy worm (with a grown-up's help, if necessary) onto the clothespin and "casting" it over the barrier. Keep other children a good distance away so they don't get bonked. The character behind the barrier removes the gummy worm and replaces it with one of the treats. (You can reuse the same small batch of gummy worms.)

Kids three to five: Keep things straightforward. Once the worm is replaced with the treat, give a tug. Then encourage the little fisherman to reel in his prize.

Kids five to seven: Make things a little more exciting. Use a heavy cord on the fishing pole so you can give kids a fight reeling in their catch. Mix "good" prizes, like a small pack of crayons, with bogus stuff, like an old grungy-looking sock.

Adaptomatic: You can make this work for any party with a water or outdoorsy theme, such as mermaids, camping, sports. Or just fudge it—have a beauty parlor party, then send the girls fishing for compliments.

DANGLING FOOD. This is such a popular staple at Halloween parties that it deserves to be played much more often. Tie a cord clothesline-style across the length of the room or area where the party is—it should be at least five feet off the ground. Have your birthday child stand under the clothesline. Measure another piece of cord so that when one end is tied to the clothesline, it ends just under your child's chin. Use this cord length as a guide for cutting more cords of equal and slightly longer length—there should be as many as there are children who will be attending the party (plus a couple extra for good measure). Tie these strings equidistant from each other along the clothesline. Before the guests arrive, tie a powdered donut to the end of each string. At some point during the party, ask each child to stand in front of a donut and put their hands behind their backs. Then let them all do their best to eat the donut off the string. Take lots of Polaroid pictures and play music throughout. Hand out goofy awards for the powder-iest face, the fastest donut eater, etc.

Ages three to five: Have lots of extra donuts on hand to replace donuts that fall off the string too quickly.

Ages five to eight: Spice things up by blindfolding the kids before they go at it.

Adaptomatic: If you're having any kind of space, alien, or science party, tie the floating food in with the whole "antigravity" concept. For an under-the-sea or water-themed or sports party—conjure up the "fishing concept" by tying gummy worms onto the strings. If the party takes place anytime in the fall, tie apples by their stem to the string and see who can take a bite of these babies first. Use Christmas cookies at Christmas, etc.

BODY DOUBLES. Outline each guest's body on a long piece (or a few long pieces) of kraft paper or butcher paper that's taped onto your driveway or to a wall, the floor, or a plastic tarp that's covering the floor inside. Let the kids fill in the picture. Award prizes for the funniest, prettiest, scariest, etc. Cut the finished art out and let your guests take it home.

Basic materials: Kraft or butcher paper, permanent ink black marker, plastic tarp, masking tape, crayons, colored markers, paint (optional—can be messy and may take time to dry), glue sticks, yarn (for hair), fabric remnants, miscellaneous junk and odds and ends for decorating.

Ages three to four: A grown-up should help the kids draw in basic facial and body features. Stick with crayons, stickers, glitter sticks, and markers here so things don't get too gloppy.

Ages five to eight: Add interesting props and materials that can be taped on for 3-D effects. The older the children are, the more free reign they should have.

Adaptomatic: If you're having a ballerina party, trace each little girl's body in a different dance position, then supply lots of tulle in sherbet hues for that all-important tutu touch. If the party has an alien theme, have guests pose in "crazy alien" positions, then give them green markers, aluminum foil—and of course, pipe cleaners for antennae—and let them create their monstrous alter egos. Slightly older girls can pose as models, then doll up their "dummies" with a fashion design that's all their own.

PHOTO BOXES. Buy a bunch of small wooden boxes at the craft or hobby store and some paints, gewgaws, and adhesives that are good for decorating them (ask a salesperson for recommendations). Take Polaroid pictures or print out digital pictures of each guest at the party. Each child decorates her box, then glues their photo onto the top of the box (an adult should help with this by tracing the outline of the box top on the back of the picture and cutting it out, if necessary).

Ages four and up: The older the children are, the longer they will be able to focus on decorating their boxes.

Adaptomatic: Be creative with the shape of the box and the possible items it can hold—choose decorating materials accordingly. For a girl, it can be a jewelry, bead, or trinket box. For a boy, the box can hold trading cards. (Yes, we're gender stereotyping.) The picture that goes on top can go with the theme, too—shoot their girls in their tutus if it's a ballerina party, have the kids wear their plastic fire hats if it's a firehouse party, etc.

PAINT-YOUR-OWN ANYTHING. Get beyond the T-shirt. Scour hobby stores for other wearable or usable canvases. Let the children decorate with fabric paint or pens, or just plain old permanent ink markers.

Ages three to four: Stick with inexpensive "canvases," such as cardboard folders or plain cardboard puzzle pieces you can buy precut at hobby stores. Have the children decorate with stamps and sponges and paints.

Ages five to eight: If the focus of the party is on creating something truly lovely, get over yourself. This is controlled helter-skelter, not Brownies, so if all they want to do is blob Elmer's glue on the palms of their hands, so be it. Arm the kids with fast-drying fabric paints and let them have a ball. If you go the T-shirt route, be sure to place cardboard inside any T-shirt you decorate so the color doesn't seep through to the back. Ask at your local craft store for more tips.

Adaptomatic: Depending on the party theme or the time of year, buy each a blank child-size apron, tool belt, or tote bag. Or provide some theme-oriented tools—for a nature-oriented party, you might provide stencils that have a leaf and flower theme. Oh yeah, and then add candy.

Chill-Out Activities and Backup Ideas

STORY TIME. Don't underestimate how much three- and four-year-old children enjoy sitting down for a story—even at a party. (After that age, you'd have to tie them up first.) It's the perfect way to give them a rest between activities or wind things down if the scene is getting wild. Let your birthday child pick a couple of favorites beforehand or buy some new books together (it's fun if they fit the theme). At the party, you sit on a chair while the children sit in front of you on the floor or ground. Do your best to give a lively read and remember to turn the book around so the kids can see the pictures—if you don't, they'll probably remind you to since they're used to this from school.

Ages two to four: If your child's up for it put her right on your lap while you read.

Ages five to eight: You won't have a prayer with this crowd unless you're telling ghost stories with the shades drawn, or reading something really, really silly.

PUZZLE RACES. If you don't already have a heap of puzzles in your house, borrow a bunch from Girlfriends or buy a handful—they're great to have on hand anyway. Choose puzzles that are geared for the same age range and have about the same number of pieces. There should be one puzzle for every two or three children. To buy some time, have the kids write their names down on pieces of paper. Toss the papers into a pillowcase or a hat, then pull names out to form teams. Hand one puzzle to each team, have them find a spot for themselves. When you say go, the race begins. Keep music going, bring in the snacks. Award a prize to the team who finishes first.

Ages four to five: Use big-piece floor puzzles—twenty to thirty pieces are about right. If these go quickly, rotate the puzzles among the teams.

Ages six to eight: Give 'em something challenging—sixty pieces might see you straight through to cake time.

MEMORY TRAY. Grab a bunch of small items—they can tie in with the theme or be just plain random. Put them on a tray and cover the tray with a towel. Have the partyers sit down on the floor and tell them you are going to show them a number of things and they should try to memorize what's on there. Pull off the towel and let the kids study the tray for a short period of time. Cover it.

Have the children write down as many objects as they can remember. The one who remembers the most, wins.

Ages five to seven: Use only about ten objects and make sure they're easy to spell. For example, a can, a top, a ball, etc. Let them study the tray for two minutes and provide spelling and writing help to those who need it.

Ages eight and up: Use fifteen or more objects. Give the kids ninety or even sixty seconds to study the tray.

SWITCH (AGES FIVE AND UP). Divide kids into two teams. Sit them across from each other on the floor. Give the children three minutes to "study" what the children on the other team are wearing. Use an egg timer to make it exciting. Now send the two teams off to different rooms and have the players on each team swap key pieces of clothes or accessories. Have a grown-up accompany each team so they can write down the changes that are made and to prevent anyone from getting too naked. Now bring the two teams back together, and have each team work together to write down what changes they see on the other team's players. The team that catches the most changes wins.

CHAPTER FIFTEEN

Parties That Worked for Us

We've given you the basics for what makes a party fun and really, that should be enough for you to go on. Just in case you're curious, though, here's a brief sampling of some of the Girlfriends' simplest and most successful birthday soirees.

Two- and Three-Year-Olds

WHO ARE THESE PEOPLE ANYWAY? Parties for two- and three-year-olds are really like a combination big playdate/mommy get-together. Two-year-olds, especially, are too young to participate in organized games. Complicated crafts are just plain silly. The key is keeping the gig short and setting up different areas of interest where the children can play at will. This is still too young for the kids to be dropped off, unless they're your nephew or next-door neighbor.

Nick's All-Red Second Birthday Party

Color is the simplest and easiest theme to work at this age. Children tend to have a favorite hue and even if they don't, colors are a concept they can grasp. Unless the color of choice is puce or ochre, the props and activities will decorate the party beautifully all by themselves. This is what our Girlfriend Lacy did for her son, Nick.

LOCATION. Backyard (can easily be done indoors).

DECORATIONS: Red streamers, balloons, plates and cups, every red child-friendly object or toy from around the house. Nick wore a plastic red fire hat he had in his toy trunk and his favorite red T-shirt.

WELCOME ACTIVITY: Nick and Lacy greeted each child and parent with a nice-sized red ball. Parent and child head for a communal table with black Sharpies where they write the child's name and add a few decorative swirls. All Sharpies returned to Party Mom after last party guest personalizes his ball.

MAIN ACTIVITIES: Activity stations included a Play-Doh table topped with chunky red balls of homemade play dough (see pg 52 for an excellent recipe), child-size rolling pins, cookie cutters, etc. Another table was topped with tiny brown-paper gift bags (Oriental Trading Company)—red markers, different shades of red crayons, red stickers, etc. Each child decorated a bag. The kids kicked and threw their red balls around the yard. The sandbox was open—mom threw in some red plastic drink cups and whatever red trucks or sand toys she had around the house. Lots of Nick's big toys—such as his pretend tool bench and trucks—were scattered around the party area for good measure.

REFRESHMENTS: Simple lunch. White frosted cake with red writing and red flowers; *no* red drinks; big bowl of cut strawberries.

CHILL TIME: Storytime—Lacy read a couple of Clifford the Big Red Dog books. Free play.

SEND-OFF: The children got their decorated favor bags and were sent off to find red lollipops and chocolate hearts covered in red foil that mom had hidden around the backyard.

FAVORS: The red candies from the treasure hunt and the red ball the children were given at the start of the party.

Three-Year-Old Sarah's Princess Jasmine Extravaganza

Our Girlfriend Sam threw this shindig for her princess-obsessed daughter, Sarah. The party had quite a number of children who were a year older and a year younger than the birthday girl. All the kids—with help from parents—got into the act and had a great time.

LOCATION: Family room, finished basement.

DECORATIONS: Several large gem-colored floor pillows from Cost Plus, finger cymbals for everyone in a basket by the door. Solid colored sheets hung in doorways and along walls to create that Casbah effect.

WELCOME ACTIVITY: The girls came in and decorated their own sheer belly dancing "panels" (harem pants, loosely translated). Sam had bought yards of various colors of cheap sheer chiffon-like fabric and hemmed one end of each Jasmine-sized piece so that she could run a drawstring through two pieces for each girl. She provided notions (an old-fashioned word for buttons and bows) that came sewn on a ribbon of fabric or could easily glue on with fabric glue.

PRELIMINARY MAIN EVENT: Sam got a teenaged niece sophisticated in the way of makeup to paint exotic cat's-eye eyeliner and light pink lip gloss on each princess. Avoid using the same brushes with each girl to limit the passing of bacteria—you can buy these cheap individual applicators at a drugstore or a beauty supply store.

MAIN EVENT: Perched in a group on their floor pillows and assorted mats, each girl (or group of girls) got a turn to stand up and do a Princess Jasmine dance. Don't let them forget their finger cymbals! If shyness is a factor, you can play the soundtrack from *Aladdin* extra loud and let them dance all together. If you or a girlfriend knows how to belly dance, get up on your feet, Girlfriend! You'll love it. Don't let dad miss this incredible Kodak moment.

REFRESHMENTS: All finger food, like sandwiches, chicken fingers, and grapes that have been cut in half. Lavender cake, pink bonbons, pink lemonade punch in a big punch bowl.

CHILL TIME: The princesses all got to have their nails painted by mom and a Girlfriend. Then they sat down on the floor, and mom sat right down in front of the group with one puppet on each hand (and a few behind her back) and proceeded to do a quick retelling of *Aladdin* (she took about ten minutes to go over the story the night before).

SEND-OFF: Each girl posed for a Polaroid (could be an instant digital photo) of her in her finery and dancing her best princess dance. This worked as both a final activity and a favor-don't you just love multi-tasking?

FAVORS: The girls got to keep their princess outfits, their pictures, and an ankle bracelet picked up from Pier One (the ones that sound like bells are the best).

Four-Year-Olds

WHO ARE THESE PEOPLE ANYWAY? Four-year-olds may seem raring to go it on their own but take it from the Girlfriends—they really do need to have their own grown-up along at the party with them. You definitely will not want to be stuck baby-sitting one miserable guest while the rest of the gang takes over the house. You'll want a bit more structure to this party, in terms of games and activities, but don't go for anything too complicated like a relay race or an art project that requires following specific directions. The kids aren't going to get it and the parents will end up doing it themselves. Obviously, not the point.

Four-Year-Old Zane's Outta-Sight Outer Space Party

Our Girlfriend Pam put on this extravaganza for her son Zane and his eighteen preschool classmates. She got the big cardboard boxes from an appliance store's Dumpster—with the manager's permission.

LOCATION: First floor of Pam's house.

DECORATIONS: Pam spray painted a washing machine–size cardboard box white and decorated it simply on the outside to look like a NASA space shuttle. She spray painted the interior black and tied and taped found objects (old CDs, an egg timer, bottle caps, styrofoam cutouts, etc.) to the interior sides so they looked like a control panel. Pam laid another refrigerator-size cardboard box on its side and covered it with a few blankets and dubbed it "The Black Hole." Black streamers were draped around the rooms. "Antigravity" gummy worms, tied to long strings, were suspended from the ceiling through the party space. Eerie space music wafted from the CD player. Lights were kept low, but Pam had scored by finding a bunch of cheap little flashlights in the Oriental Trading Company catalog. Pam made mock "space helmets" for the kids to share by covering two kid-size football helmets she had around the house with aluminum foil. She wrote NASA on the side of each one with a Sharpie, then hid the pen in her jewelry box.

WELCOME ACTIVITY: Pam and Zane directed each guest to a table where they found a cardboard cutout in the shape of a space shuttle with their name on it. They then sat down and decorated their space shuttles with feathers, glitter, and other crafts paraphernalia Pam had placed in containers down the center of a large folding table.

THE MAIN EVENT: The children lined up with their shuttles and took turns taping them to a large piece of black spray-painted cardboard that had various planets painted on it. Sort of "pin the shuttle on the planet" without blindfolds. Next, they headed off to the "space room" where they had a blast playing with the space shuttle and "Black Hole." Pam's husband sat on a stool outside the shuttle and played "mission control," using the microphone portion of a kiddie tape recorder. The kids also had free reign to create space graffiti on the space shuttle with washable markers Pam had set out for them. There were also a couple of blow-up aliens, which the kids had a blast whacking around.

REFRESHMENTS: While the kids played, Pam cleaned off the crafts tables and set them up for snack. She served: Planet Cakes—four single-layer round cakes, frosted in different colors with craters done in darker hues. Mini plastic astronauts were perched on top (and quickly removed once the candles went out so no one would choke). Chips, pretzels, juice.

CHILL TIME: Pam asked each child to stand next to one of the worms that was hanging around the room. When she signaled "go," the children all raced to nibble the worm off the string. She gave out prizes to the fastest, funniest, slowest, etc., worm eaters. This turned out to be so amusing that Pam and the other parents ended up tying more gummy worms and practically every other type of food at the party onto the strings, so the children raced to nibble them off. As various guests tired of this activity, they returned to the space room for more mayhem.

SEND-OFF: Pam had all the guests collect their things and put on their coats. She gave each child their favor bag, then ushered them out the front door where a space shuttle piñata was dangling from a tree. Once the thing exploded and the kids stuffed the candy into their favor bags, it was "ta-ta!"

FAVORS: Pam filled silver Mylar bags with the space shuttle each child had made, a small bag of Sun Chips, and a sheet of solar system window decals.

Five-Year-Olds

WHO ARE THESE PEOPLE ANYWAY? The good news here is that kids are usually ready to go solo at parties, so you won't need to feed their parents or embarrass yourself in front of them. The bad news is that these little people are all yours to entertain. To avoid tears at all costs, stick with simple, not-so-competitive games and activities.

Ellie's Five-Year-Old Backyard Splash

Shelli wrote on the invitation that, if the weather was nice, guests should wear their bathing suits under their clothes and bring a towel. She reminded parents about this when they (or Shelli) RSVP'd. Shelli also had big T-shirts on hand for the kids to use as painting smocks, plus extra bathing suits, towels, and sunblock just in case. If it had rained, Shelli had every intention of sending the kids outside anyway. We all still wonder if she was serious.

LOCATION: Shelli's backyard.

DECORATIONS: Shelli dangled lots of blue, green, and turquoise streamers from the trees and tied helium balloons of the same colors to the fences and chairs. She wrote "Welcome to Ellie's Birthday Splash" on a six-foot-long piece of white kraft paper and drew some basic "ocean" shapes, such as starfish, seaweed, coral, and fish on it. Then she taped it to the backyard fence. The table was set in blues and greens.

WELCOME ACTIVITY: Shelli purchased a bunch of sponge-type paint-brushes at the hardware store. Ellie handed out paintbrushes to her friends as they arrived and pointed them toward the mural, where paints and old T-shirt smocks awaited.

MAIN EVENT: Shelli had all sorts of watery activities set up for fun. She handed out empty spray bottles, which she had labeled beforehand with each child's name. She showed the children how to fill them up in the kiddy pool, then let them go nuts. There was a "fishing station" set up, where kids took turns fishing for treats. Shelli also set out a Slip'n Slide and every water toy her family owned. Kids who didn't feel like joining the melee continued to paint the mural or popped over to Shelli's mom, who was doing some simple face painting and temporary tattooing.

REFRESHMENTS: Simple lunch. Shelli purchased a cake with a mermaid "painted" on it from her supermarket.

CHILL TIME: Shelli purchased small, natural sea sponges in bulk over the Internet (www.craftbear.com/ageansponge, just in case you're wondering). She set them out with some tempera paints poured into shallow dishes and had the children "sponge paint" some inexpensive foam frames she purchased at the craft store.

SEND-OFF: Shelli sent all the kids off on a hunt for big, industrial-size sponges (same Internet source as above) she had hidden around the backyard. When all of the sponges were found, the games began. The girls had a soaked-sponge toss. Shelli also set up a relay with a full bucket on one end and an empty one on the other. The two teams each raced to soak a sponge, race across the yard, squeezed it out in the empty bucket, race back and hand it to the next player. The whole thing was such a hoot, it turned into a giant water fight with the soaking wet sponges being the operative weapon. Once everyone was soaked and pooped, the kids got changed and headed home.

FAVORS: Each friend went home with their own spray bottle, and a gallon-size Ziploc into which Shelli had placed a small Ziploc filled with Swedish fish, a mini bottle of bubble bath, a clean sea sponge, and one of the cleaned sponge paintbrushes they had used earlier in the party.

Six- and Seven-Year-Olds
Who are these people anyway?

Six- and seven-year-olds have got the party thing down. They arrive expecting good fun, good loot, and good food. Be prepared to keep them busy and have lots of extra activities up your sleeve.

Sasha's Pop Star Party

All three of our Girlfriend Amanda's children were born during the winter, so she's become an expert at throwing indoor parties. Here's what she did for her daughter Sasha and about eight of her girlfriends.

LOCATION: Inside, first floor and basement of the house.

DECORATIONS: Amanda had rented a disco ball from a party supply store, like a Regal Rents, and hung it from the middle of the ceiling. She replaced any incandescent lightbulbs with colored ones and bought Mylar streamers and a few Mylar balloons to give it that authentic disco feel. She also borrowed a $200 karaoke machine from the nine-year-old she used to baby-sit before she had kids of her own.

WELCOME ACTIVITY: Amanda loaded up on cheap sunglasses, jewelry, feather boas, and plenty of lipstick and face glitter. She let the girls design their own costumes with the stuff, reserving the lipstick application for her own experienced hand. The girl actually singing got to wear the most coveted item, an outrageous feather-trimmed cape (left over from the Halloween Mom went as Elton John), then passed it along to the next little diva.

MAIN ACTIVITIES: Encouraging the girls to sing alone, with a friend, in a quartet or as a group, they started singing karaoke songs. Trust us, kids know the words to every Disney ditty by heart. After the ice is broken the girls become microphone hogs and are much braver in the limelight. Make a video and take lots of Polaroids.

REFRESHMENTS: Ginger ale in fancy plastic glasses. The cake, which Mom ordered from the supermarket, featured an exact image of Sasha's head atop a groovily garbed body in hip clothes and holding a microphone.

CHILL TIME: Dad hooked up the video camera to the TV in the family room (after searching for the connecting cables for two hours the night before) and showed the giggling girls their performances. Every parent who came to pick up was dragged in by her child "just to see *my* part, Mom."

FAVORS: Silver foil–wrapped chocolate stars, the sunglasses, feather boas, lots of Polaroids. Sasha sent along a dupe of the karaoke video with each thank-you—a nice touch, but not a must.

Seven-Year-Olds

WHO ARE THESE PEOPLE ANYWAY? Well, it all depends on whether we're talking about boys, girls, or a combination of both. Boys will start running the minute their feet make traction, and the girls will generally wait in small chatty groups before getting into the swing of things. If you have both boys and girls, with minor exceptions, you're throwing two parallel parties, one for each gender. It won't surprise you to learn we suggest you stick to your birthday child's gender and cut yourself some slack.

Jeff's Baseball Party

Our Girlfriend Jenny threw this party for her son Jeff and about thirteen other boys. On the invitation, she encouraged athletic moms and dads to come play, if they cared to. She also mentioned that the boys could bring their mitts if they had them, *but no bats would be necessary, thank you.*

LOCATION: Make sure you check with Parks and Rec before scheduling a party on their turf—they often have a reservation policy or will want to share interesting information, like the toilets are broken.

DECORATIONS: Almost none, except for balloons and some baseball banners and paraphernalia from around the house. The big prep work was done by Jenny's husband, Marc. Using a permanent ink marker, Marc drew the New York Yankees logo on the front of eight plain white T-shirts and the New York Mets logo on the front of eight plain white T-shirts. (Remember, you can also pick up team T-shirts pretty inexpensively at a local sporting goods store.) He also ordered a CD of *Baseball's Greatest Hits* from the National Baseball Hall of Fame and brought a battery-operated boom box to the park (with eight extra batteries).

WELCOME ACTIVITIES: Jenny had bought several Wiffle balls and plastic bats for the kids to knock around while awaiting their team members. Marc also brought a baseball so he could play catch with the kids who showed up with mitts and knew how to use them.

MAIN ACTIVITIES: Marc led a Simon Says–style team warmup. Then all the boys were spread out in a semicircle just a little closer to home plate than at a Little League game. Marc led them in a game of Three Strikes and You're Out with his pal Hal (another daddy) playing the critical role of catcher.

REFRESHMENTS: A lot of liquids, all stashed in a cooler along the third-base line. Hot dogs that were boiled at home and kept warm in an insulated bag plus all the fixin's because kids this age are starting to like relish and mustard and even sauerkraut. A sheet cake from the local grocery story with baseball decorations taken right out of their sample book. Boxes of Cracker Jack, of course.

CHILL TIME: After Jenny and Marc get the boys to sit down on the grass they opened up a big box (the ones that are about a foot long) of baseball cards and let the gang go rummaging.

SEND-OFF: Jeff handed out baseball-themed favor bags filled with baseball cards, a pack of that bubble gum that's looks like a pro player's chewing tobacco, and one of those pens or pencils from the catalogs that have the teams names on them. If you can find small rubber balls painted like baseballs you might throw one of those in, too.

Eight-Year-Olds

WHO ARE THESE PEOPLE? They're basically seven-year-olds with 50 percent more manual dexterity, 50 percent more energy, 50 percent more vocabulary, and 50 percent shorter attention spans.

Jeremy's Eighth Birthday Backyard Campout

Vicki threw this party for her son's birthday, and believe us, it's the closest most of them ever came to roughing it.

LOCATION: Family's backyard, except to use the toilet.

DECORATIONS: One big rented tent that could sleep ten kids each, if this were a sleepover, which it wasn't. A low charcoal barbecue, which served as a pretend campfire (Dad was stationed there all night). Long tables were covered in plasticized red-and-white check tablecloths with battery-operated lanterns on each one. A rope tied between two trees to suspend a rustic sign that said Camp Jeremy. Each camper was also given a small flashlight, which came in handy during the scary stories.

REFRESHMENTS: Grilled hot dogs and hamburgers (if you have to hire someone to watch the little "campfire" while you and dad do the serious cooking on the Weber, it shouldn't cost more than twenty-five dollars.) Canned baked beans, corn on the cob, and root beer (sarsaparilla!).

WELCOME ACTIVITY: Each arrival was dragged into a ferocious-but-fun game of tug-o-war; Vicki assigned sides as each boy entered the backyard.

MAIN EVENT: If your mate is a scary storyteller from way back, have the kids gather around the low barbecue while he spins some spooky yarns. If he can't remember them all, there are lots of books in the library and in bookstores or on-line (try www.castleofspirits.com) to refresh his memory, since they haven't changed in forty years. After he's exhausted his bag of tricks, encourage him to let anyone in the crowd offer up their scariest story.

WINDING DOWN: Bring out the birthday cake—the candles will be the main attraction if the sun has started setting. And then, yup, you guessed it—it's time for s'mores and roasted marshmallows (let grown-ups handle the roasting chores to avoid any burn hazards).

FAVORS: Vicki went to an army-navy store and stocked up on old-fashioned kerchief scarves. Inside each one were three or four pieces of favorite candies, like Twizzlers, Hot Rocks, and Sour Bites, as well as inedible treats like those rods you crack in the middle and they glow for the rest of the night. Any Polaroids during the scary storytime were stashed in there, too.

Need Space?

Let's say you want to stage a party yourself but don't have the space or intestinal fortitude to do it on your own turf. Here are some alternatives the Girlfriends have scrounged up over the years:

Girl Scout Houses: Those little troopers own some pretty darned impressive real estate—rustic cabins out in the woods, houses, and condos in the heart of town. In many cases, they'll rent out the space to you for the day or overnight—even if you've never so much as considered earning a badge. For local contact info, log on at www.girlscouts.org.

Community Centers and Local Ys: Community centers rent out rooms for meetings and kids' parties at bargain prices. Often the fee includes the use of tables, chairs, and basic kitchen facilities. You're usually responsible for cleaning up.

Hotel Rooms: This is possibly the best-kept secret in the birthday world—and the perfect setup for a girls' mock or full-fledged slumber party. Front desk folks at those big chain hotels will often rent a hotel room to a smallish flock, then look the other way while the group orders in pizza, swims in the indoor pool, or hangs out in the game room. The key here is following the rules—such as no food at the pool—and not making a racket. Basically, think in terms of girls seven and up (even older, if swimming is involved since lifeguards generally aren't on duty). Our Girlfriend Kerry, who has exercised the hotel option more than once—strongly recommends the all-suite or extended-stay hotels that generally cater to business people. They tend to clear out on the weekends and the kitchens are a super-handy plus. She actually rents adjoining rooms, allows four girls to sleep in one and hangs out with a mommy Girlfriend in the other.

Local Playgrounds and Play Fields: Get the most out of your tax dollars—set up shop at one of your town playgrounds or parks. Check with your town hall to see if you need to reserve the space or pay a permit fee. Choose a spot that has a convenient bathroom, and ideally, a lean-to or pavillion, so you and the gang have some shelter from drizzles or searing sun.

The Local Firehouse: What exactly these guys will do for *you* depends upon the policy in your town and how well you can sweet-talk them. Give a call to the fire chief's office and see where it gets you. Our Girlfriend Connie persuaded the fire truck to come to her at-home firehouse party. (She didn't tell Pierce a thing about the special appearance, in case the truck had some hot business to attend to.) Our Girlfriend Gwen walked a dozen four-year-old boys to the firehouse near her home, they climbed all over the truck and met the fire guys, then Gwen walked them over to the pizzeria down the street for lunch. The most impressive deal by far: In our Girlfriend Helen's town, the fire guys give a full tour of the firehouse, conduct a mini fire safety lesson (complete with stop, drop, and roll), and let the kids picnic in their dining room, to boot. None of this should cost a penny, though it's nice to bring some lunch—or at least some Danish along—as a way of saying thanks. Also remember, if there's a fire, you're pretty much up a creek.

CHAPTER SIXTEEN

It's Her Party and I'll Pay If I Want To: Party Places and Other Sanity-Saving Options

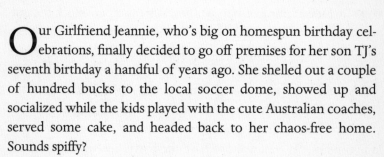

Our Girlfriend Jeannie, who's big on homespun birthday celebrations, finally decided to go off premises for her son TJ's seventh birthday a handful of years ago. She shelled out a couple of hundred bucks to the local soccer dome, showed up and socialized while the kids played with the cute Australian coaches, served some cake, and headed back to her chaos-free home. Sounds spiffy?

Jeannie was miserable. She whined that it was just too easy. She kvetched that it wasn't personal enough. She felt guilty about the expense. She did so, of course, until TJ informed her that he had a complete blast and begged to do it again for his next birthday. No stress. No clean up. No damage. Happy child. Who was she to argue?

The Girlfriends will say it one more time:

Pain and suffering is not a required part of the party formula.

If your child wants a party that's easy and affordable, if a bit prosaic, let her have it. If you don't want to do the homespun party
thing, you are not cheating your child. If you emerge from the
whole affair rested, happy, and solvent, it doesn't mean something went wrong.

The really cool part is that all roads don't necessarily lead to
Chuck E. Cheese or that chaotic play zone you're so sick of.
These days, there are oodles of non-migraine-inducing alterna-
tives out there and many are surprisingly affordable. Here's the
Girlfriends' lowdown on some of the obvious and not-so-obvious
party possibilities:

BOWLING ALLEYS: A good, no-work option for kids six and up. Any
younger and they won't be able to lift the ball or will be tempted
to wander down the lanes. Many places offer affordable packages
that include a round of bumper bowling (bumpers block the gutters so it's less frustrating for the kiddies) and lunch. Take it from
the Girlfriends, though, a bowling alley is not a bowling alley is
not a bowling alley. Many have a wholesome family-friendly feel.
We've been to some, though, where the smoke was so thick the
kids couldn't see the pins and big, burly bowling dudes started
hitting on the moms. Pay a visit to the lanes you're considering at
the time of day you want to have the party. See what the vibe is
like. Also be sure to check out where they plan to be serving the
kids lunch. Next to the bar, obviously, is not ideal.

PAINT-YOUR-OWN CERAMICS STUDIOS: For a small group of girls, especially, carefully decorating a piggy bank or plate, while sipping
pink lemonade, is a lovely way to spend an afternoon or even an
early evening. The key here is not jumping the gun. Kids younger
than seven slop the paint on their ceramics in a matter of minutes—then, generally, there ain't much for anyone to do except

trash the place and harass other customers. Keep in mind, also, that the ceramics aren't ready to take home at the end of the party, which means you've usually got to pick them up after they're fired and hand deliver them.

GYMNASTICS STUDIOS: Gymnastics for very young children has nothing to do with wearing pastel leotards and working out on uneven parallel bars. It's more about bouncing off padded walls and jumping around a lot in wide-open spaces. What could be more perfect for a crowd of little rabble-rousers? Check out gymnastics studios in the area and see what kind of party packages they offer. Try to meet the person who will be instructing the party—you'll want someone who's energetic and upbeat and who understands that the event should be fun, not a mini boot camp for Olympic competition.

MUSEUMS: Children's museums are an excellent and obvious choice, but don't limit yourself. Lots of fine art, natural history, and science museums offer children's party packages with excellent hands-on activities and instruction. Also consider some of the small, offbeat cultural institutions out there—railroad museums, doll museums, police museums, naval and aviation museums, agricultural and wildlife museums, building museums. Whatever your area lays claim to, chances are they do parties and the prices are reasonable. If you have no idea of what's around, check out www.museumspot.com or just type "museums"+ the name of your state, into your search engine on the Internet and see what comes up.

CHILDREN'S THEATERS AND PUPPET THEATERS: In many cases this is a relatively pricey proposition—especially if you take over the whole theater, which is the nicest way to go. To make the concept more affordable, opt for a small theater—the kids won't be too picky if it's a little less professional.

CHILDREN'S ART STUDIOS: Another excellent, if pricey, party option. See if the instructor can theme her art projects according to your child's interests of the moment—dinosaurs, gardening, sports, animals, etc.

ZOOS, AQUARIUMS, ETC: Lots of these places offer party packages, which usually include group admission and the use of a room for lunch and cake. Some go all out by providing special group activities, a host or tour guide, and lunch. If you want to keep costs down, choose a zoo or aquarium that has an open picnic or lunch area, take a small group on your own, and serve lunch to them yourself. Check ahead of time what the minimum number is to qualify your group for a discount. Tip: Have a grown-up claim a couple of tables and stay with them while the kids roam and have fun. When it's time for lunch, you won't want to be hunting for seats with a gaggle of hungry partiers on your heels.

NATURE CENTERS: If you have an environmental education center, an Audubon Society, an arboretum, or nature reserve nearby, check in with them and see if they allow parties on premises. Even if they don't offer formal packages, you may be able to arrange for a naturalist or child educator to take the kids around or lead a nature hike. Ask if you can bring along cake and a picnic—and if there's a place you can hunker down for lunch indoors if it rains.

BAKERIES: There's a bakery where our friend Liz lives that puts on fabulous—though pricey—parties for kids of all ages. The junior bakers are each given aprons and taken back into the kitchen. First, the birthday child decorates her own cake, with the help of the pastry chef. Then everyone gets to work at their own baking station, where they roll out and cut the dough for sugar cookies. After a pizza bagel lunch, the kids get to decorate their baked cookies with a huge array of confections. The masterpieces are then wrapped up in a white bakery box and sent home as favors. We admit, it's a long shot that the bakery near you is doing anything like this. But it's worth checking into—perhaps they'll be inspired (and adequately insured) to give it a shot.

TOURIST TRAINS: If you've got a train nut on your hands, consider taking a group for a ride on a historic steam train. These dramatic iron behemoths are scattered around the country; many are affiliated with rail museums. In same cases, you can purchase a formal party package, complete with a private caboose for the occasion. To find out what's in your area, check out the Tourist Trains section at www.routesinternational.com.

PICK-YOUR-OWN FRUIT AND VEGETABLE FARMS: Why not haul a bunch of kids out to a "pick-your-own" place and have a blast filling "favor" baskets with whatever's in season—blueberries, strawberries, pumpkins, apples. Some of the bigger farms have additional kid pleasers like hayrides, baby animals, and mini-tractors at "pickers" disposal, often for no extra cost. Check with the owners in advance, but you probably won't have a problem if you settle down on the grounds to picnic and play games like "Duck Duck Goose" after the picking's over. Some farms offer actual "party packages"—the Girlfriends have been to quite a few of these and they're lovely, but they'll cost you a good deal more than a few baskets of apples will. Also keep in mind: Since the Hoof and Mouth Disease scare a few years ago, some animal farms and zoos have gotten out of the whole "petting zoo" business altogether. Even if you can find a place that still does this, think twice: It may make some moms uneasy.

PLAY EQUIPMENT PLACES: Our Girlfriend Caitlin was stunned when her daughter Ann received an invitation to a birthday party at Wood Kingdom, a place out near her home that sells those big wooden swing sets and other sporting equipment. Wouldn't you know it, the gig worked out great. The kids had the run of a few spectacular play sets that were set up in a private indoor space. The party package also included a party helper, pizza lunch, treasure hunt, favors, and a magic show, to boot. If you have a play equipment place near your home, check and see if they can set something up for you (and have insurance to make it legit).

Before You Sign On for Anything . . .

- **Think out the travel logistics.** No matter how great a party place might be, few parents will be thrilled if they have to drive more than twenty minutes to reach it. If you or your child absolutely have your heart set on something that's out of the way, keep the group small (don't even consider taking children under the age of five), corral a couple of vehicles and Girlfriend drivers, and transport the clan yourself. Ask parents to bring their children's booster seats so everyone rides safely.
- **See the facility firsthand and meet the party staff.** A particular museum or pizzeria may seem like a cool place overall, but the space they use for parties could be down in a dank

corner of their basement or the party staff could consist of a couple of clueless teenagers. Make sure you check out the facilities thoroughly and that the actual party space is clean, cheerful, and at least appears to be child-safe. See where the children will be eating and what the bathrooms look like. Meet the party staff—if they're grouchy, hapless, or creepy toward you, they won't be any more charming with your children. Ask if you can pop in on a party that's similar to the one you're considering—in an ideal world, find time to actually do so.

- **Find out how they charge.** Some places charge by the head. If that's the case, how far in advance will you need to provide a head count? A lot of venues these days charge a flat fee for parties up to a certain number, say ten or fifteen, then charge by the head for anything over that amount. In the Girlfriends' experience, the best way to go in this case is to over-invite just a bit. It's better to pay a bit more for a few extras if they all show up than it is to shell out a lump sum, have last-minute cancellations, and not even come close to filling the quota.

- **Find out what's included in the package price.** Some places only include use of the facilities, a party host or hostess, and lunch. Others provide absolutely everything—all you need to do is bring warm bodies. If you're dealing with the latter, ask to see what goes in the favor bags, what they'll use for decorations, what the cake looks like. If some of these features seem junky or skimpy, see if they'll prorate the package and let you BYO.

- **Sniff out hidden costs.** Is cleanup included in the fee? Will there be a charge for extra seating or tables, if needed? Will they charge for parents who choose to stick around? Be sure also to ask about tipping. Some places automatically include gratuities in their package fee, some don't.

- **Ask for a rundown of the party agenda.** What will the children do when they arrive? What will they spend most of their time doing? If you want to personalize the party a bit, see if the party staff can incorporate some of your child's favorite games or interests into the schedule. For example, if your daughter's totally into penguins and you're planning the event at an aquarium, ask the party person if the host can spend extra time in the penguin area. If games are on the agenda, ask which ones: Should the list include something your child detests—musical chairs immediately comes to mind—pleasantly ask them to make a substitution.

- **Determine how "private" your party will be.** Inquire if other parties will be taking place at the same time as yours. If so, ask how the party staff controls the frenzy and makes each group feel important. Will there be a designated staff person in charge of your particular party? Will your group have its own room for cake? Are activities and tours staggered so you won't end up trampling each other—or losing track of your guests?

- **Check those references.** If you or a Girlfriend haven't actually attended a party at a particular place, ask the manager for a few references and be sure to call them. Even if the reference is the owner's sister, a few carefully crafted questions should give you a good feel for the place. Is there a particular party host you should request or avoid? What was the highlight of the party? What did the staff do to personalize the party for the birthday child? How did the staffers deal with children who weren't participating or were misbehaving?

How did the cake taste? Is there anything you'd ask them to do differently next time?

- **Ask about their cancellation policy.** In most cases, you'll forfeit your deposit. The most charitable folks will allow you to apply that money toward a future date. Should you be considering a place that's outdoors or that has an outdoor component, find out what they do when it rains. Do they have a plan B? Do they plod on, regardless of the raindrops? Do they postpone? Do they provide party moms with umbrellas and Valium?

CHAPTER SEVENTEEN

When You and Your Child Are the Guests

As the Girlfriends have said before, birthday parties are a two-way street. We parents of young children not only throw parties. We also wind up attending them—or dispatching our children to them—on a near constant basis during their younger years. Here, some dos and don'ts for Girlfriendly party-going:

- Do RSVP—think about how much easier you'll make life for the host mom.

- Don't do a "no-show." If your child is sick or there's an urgent problem, of course you should call the host mom and cancel. But don't simply bag the event if something more interesting comes up or you decide you'd rather linger over the Sunday papers. There's a child who wants your child to be at her birthday party. It would be a real shame to disappoint her (and very possibly, your child, too).

- Don't bring siblings (unless they aren't walking yet and will thus be in your arms the entire time or if the host mom suggests it). If you have no choice, ask ahead of time and—if the party is at a "party place"—make it clear that the sibling does not need to participate (in which case you're better off not bringing them anyway).

- Do dress your child with fun in mind. Unless the invitation is for high tea at The Plaza, skip the dry-clean-only dresses and hand-knit sweaters. Think cute, comfortable, and easy to clean. Clean sneakers always make a good impression, however, as does freshly shampooed and combed hair.

- Whenever possible, do request a "gift" receipt when you buy the present and give it along with the gift. It won't have the price on it but will allow the birthday girl to return what you've given her if she already has it (or simply doesn't dig it).

- Never regift. Call it a mom's sixth sense, but almost all of us can detect a gift that's been recycled. There was one lightsaber that our Girlfriend Tula swears made the rounds of at least five parties in her town. You'll be better off buying something small and thoughtful and giving your excess stuff to charity.

- Do show up on time. Fashionably late doesn't cut it here. Children's birthday parties are short as it is and it really can take away from the activities if everyone trickles in little by little. Your child may also feel left out or uncomfortable if she arrives after the fun has already begun, plus the goodies may be gone and the moonbounce deflated.

- Don't be late for pickup. The host mom won't appreciate it and neither will your child.

• Do stick around with your younger child. Even if your little one is accustomed to drop-off playdates, you should stay with him at a party if he's four or younger. Kids this young are simply too unpredictable and dependent for a host parent to watch single-handedly. There's also no telling how your child might react to a big crowd and she may wind up crying—and on the host mom's lap—for the duration of the party. This is definitely not a good way for you or your child to win friends. As your child gets a bit older, take parties on a case-by-case basis and if you have doubts, play it safe and lurk in the background unobtrusively. By the age of about five, most kids are ready to go the party circuit solo.

The Gift Horse

With all these parties to attend, birthday present buying can become a full-time job and a financial fiasco. To make matters worse, half the time you feel like you're buying just another piece of junk that will be abandoned in the toy box after only a matter of days.

Don't fret. Having given and received countless presents, the Girlfriends now know how to please birthday children *and their parents* without sacrificing our own children's college tuition in the process.

First things first: Where to get all these goodies. The Girlfriends' big shopping tip here is, "don't limit yourself to toy stores." Of course, they're a good bet, especially when you're buying for relatively young children. However, when kids get older (five and up, let's say), there are many gifts they'll love that aren't toys at all, and you'll find them in all kinds of convenient and affordable places. Here's where the Girlfriends go gift hunting:

The Usual Suspects

TOY SUPERSTORES: Namely, Toys "Я" Us (and for babes about three and under, Babies "Я" Us) and Kaybee's (at least in some cities) are where you're going to find all the stuff that's advertised during Saturday morning cartoons. Certainly there's no shortage of pink and purple plastic junk, but it's also the logical and budget-friendly source for much loved mass-market basics like Matchbox cars, Little Tikes, Lego sets, Barbies galore, and everything Fisher-Price. Toys "Я" Us has recently gobbled up Imaginarium, so it's possible to find some of the more upscale stuff you find in the specialty stores there as well.

SPECIALTY CHAINS: Zany Brainy, Learning Express, and other toy stores of their "educational" ilk carry some of the big-name basics plus many smaller and high-end brands you won't generally find at the mass-market operations. Some of the names you'll see a lot of are Brio, Small World Toys, Battat, Chicco, and Learning Resources. Don't assume that everything at these stores is "better" for kids than what you'll find at mass merchandisers—often you'll find pretty much the same stuff, but with a fancier name and higher price tag attached.

TOY BOUTIQUES: These are those charming little shops in nice neighorhoods where every toy seems to be handpicked by an individual who is part toy purist, part interior decorator. Along with their selection of good stuff from boutiquey toy makers like Schylling and Montgomery Schoolhouse, you'll also often encounter a variety of handmade and high-minded items real kids couldn't give a hoot about. Shop carefully.

INTERNET TOY BOUTIQUES: The Girlfriends simply adore browsing for funky and not-so-funky toys on the Internet. We just don't do much small-time birthday present buying because we generally don't work far enough in advance and it's not worth paying for shipping (unless the birthday child doesn't live near us). Considering how fleeting Internet toy retailers seem to be (may eToys rest in peace) we're not even going to attempt to mention any sites by name. Check Amazon as well as Yahoo! to see who's under their umbrella.

TOY CATALOGUES: The Girlfriends don't do much small-scale birthday present buying by catalogue for the same reasons we avoid the Internet. We do, however, love the catalogues at Christmastime and when we're buying for out-of-town friends and relatives. A couple of favorites:

Constructive Playthings, www.constplay.com, 800-448-7830, for a solid selection of toys—it's a very good source for wooden unit blocks.

Lilly's Kids, www.lillianvernon.com, 800-545-5426, an offshoot of the Lillian Vernon catalogue that's filled with affordable and not-so-usual gifts. Some of the stuff is junky but with a good eye you can scare up some cute things, like colorful cardboard building bricks, a wooden box filled with magnetic letters, handpainted wooden jewelry chests, and oodles of items they'll personalize for free, from sleep mats to lunch boxes to pencil cases.

Sensational Beginnings, www.sensationalbeginnings.com, 800-444-2147, for an excellent selection of classic toys that may be hard to find locally.

Other Terrific Sources

OFFICE SUPPLY SUPERSTORES (STAPLES, OFFICEMAX, ETC.): The children's supply section has all kinds of cool stationery sets, pen sets, stencils, stickers, and art materials. Also consider other possibilities, like an electronic change sorter, or a dry-erase board with tons of dry-erase pens.

HOUSEWARE SUPERSTORES (LINENS 'N THINGS, BED BATH & BEYOND, ETC.): Tons of stuff at these places for kids' rooms, from colorful fleece throws to twirling rice-paper lanterns that shoot whimsical silhouettes around the room. There's usually a good selection of art supplies and the front registers often have kid-friendly items on sale. (They're no dummies.)

WAREHOUSE CLUBS (COSTCO, SAM'S CLUB, BJ'S, ETC.): Books, big plastic toys, giant Crayola gift packs, DVDs, CD-ROMs, you name it. Pick up what catches your eye the next time you're shopping for diapers or paper towels and stash it in your linen closet for upcoming parties.

SPORTING GOODS STORES (THE SPORTS AUTHORITY, MODELL'S, ETC.): Our Girlfriend Nancy, who has three boys, does every bit of her birthday-present buying at these places. Of course, there are lots of kid-size balls, bats, and sports gear. But how about any thing you can possibly think of that's emblazoned with a child's favorite sports team logo—beach towels, sleeping bags, backpacks, and jerseys. How about a baseball- or football-themed chess or checkers games? Or Mets Monopoly?

FASHION/GENERAL DISCOUNTERS (DAFFY'S, MARSHALLS, ETC.): Lots of times you'll pay less for boutiquey toys and duds at these places than you will for mass-market junk you'll find at mainstream toy or clothes stores. Due to their "surplus" nature, inventories at stores like this are erratic. If you see something you like, grab it and store it. Just be sure to get a gift receipt.

CRAFT AND HOBBY STORES (RAG SHOP, A.C. MOORE, MICHAEL'S, ETC.): These stores sell crafts kits of all kinds, plus lots of wonderful crafts supplies. How about buying a child her first photo album? Or an unfinished wooden birdhouse and some paints and let him decorate it himself? There's lots to dig up here.

GENERAL DISCOUNT MERCHANDISERS: Most of our Girlfriends won't walk into a Wal-Mart or Target without doing a stroll through the toy aisle. They have great prices and are competitive with Toys "Я" Us in merchandise. Their sales on board games and select Lego and Fisher-Price play sets are wonderful, and you can get a gift receipt.

The Gift List

As the Girlfriends see it, the ideal gift for a child who is not your own, who will be getting about fifteen million other presents at the same time, and whose parents may not have the same values or housekeeping standards as you do,

- Requires little or no assembly

- Comes with batteries included (a Girlfriends' cardinal rule)

- Does not have lots of tiny pieces

- Does not press potential hot buttons with regard to violence, sex, gender, and race

- Does not breathe, eat, or poop (even if they're robo pets)

- Will not make a mess

- Requires no additional expense

Now for our nitty-gritty list of age-appropriate suggestions.

First Birthday

WHAT'S DOING: On this biggie birthday, babies are celebrating their new mobility—whether they're confidently cruising around or already strutting on their own. Along with their growing sense of independence comes the urge to explore absolutely everything with their hands and a fascination with action and reaction.

WHAT THEY LOVE: Simple push toys and ride ons are perfect now, as are easy-to-grasp balls, toys that open and close, fill-and-spill toys, lightweight blocks, and basic clutch dolls. Books are ideal in board form, with rhythmic, repetitive prose, bold graphics, and simple concepts such as bedtime and animals' names.

Your Basic Great Gifts

Skwish Ball (Pappa Gepetto): An irresistable "ball" made from black elastic cord and wooden beads that babes can squish flat, fold, bounce, or chew. A little bell in the center makes it even more charming. Available at most specialty toy stores.

Jumbo Pounding Bench (Small World): A smoother, more stylized version of the no-frills classic that's no longer made. The pegs are a little too easy to pound, in the Girlfriends' opinion, but maybe our kids are eating too many Wheaties.

ImagiBRICKS Cardboard Building Blocks (ImagiPLAY): These are the traditional cardboard blocks with the brick design you see in almost every preschool. Great as a first construction toy since no one will get hurt if the bricks go flying (which they undoubtedly will).

Duplo Primo (Lego): Even bigger and chunkier than Lego's Duplo blocks, in a handy plastic container. Serves as a first construction toy and a dump and clunk, to boot.

Taking It Up a Notch

Ready Steady Ride-On (Fisher-Price): A great, basic first set of wheels. No pedals—babes propel it Flintstone-style, by pushing their feet along the ground.

Soft, stuffed teddy bears and other potential loveys (Try the cuties from The Boyds Collection or Gund): This is the time when a babe may attach herself to that one "special" object. The one you give might be it. Be sure to choose something with sewn eyes (as opposed to plastic or glass) and an absence of other doodads that might pose a choking hazard.

Pop-Up Dinosaurs (Tolo): Baby dinosaurs hatch from colorful eggs when baby pushes, twists, and otherwise manipulates corresponding buttons. This is the latest twist on a pop-up classic.

The "Ooh, Ahh!" Gifts

Baby Hut (Playhut): A pop-up tent that's the perfect cozy size for little explorers.

Rollercoaster Bead Maze (Anatex): These are the toys you see at just about every pediatrician's office. Babes love to play with them even when they don't have an ear infection.

BOOKS: *Good Night, Gorilla; White on Black* and other color-contrast books by Tana Hoban; *The Mitten; Jesse Bear, What Will You Wear?;* and *Jamberry.*

Second Birthday

WHAT'S DOING: This is when pretend play really takes off. Toddlers at two are particularly fascinated by everything that mom and dad do . . . and they want to be part of the action. With their "me do it" approach to just about everything, babes this age are eager to learn new words and to test the waters of coloring, dancing, and music.

WHAT THEY LOVE: Plastic dishes, pretend food, doll strollers, pretend shopping carts, smooth plastic cars and trucks, and other basic props that encourage pretend pursuits. Shape sorters, stacking cubes, large-piece wooden puzzles, simple construction toys, and extra-chunky crayons help toddlers develop their fine motor skills. Letter, number, shape, and color books and those with simple story lines are best. Interactive, lift-the-flap books also thrill kids of this age.

Your Basic Great Gifts

Little Rhythmmaker Rhythm Set (Little Tikes): A pair of maracas and a tambourine made of chunky plastic. They'll last—and get play—for years.

Ernest or Emma Moody Bear Puzzle (Schylling): A tidy little wooden box with a small puzzle board and eighteen interchangeable puzzle pieces inside that allow kids to change the bear's moods and outfits. Great for keeping kids busy while on the go.

Taking It Up a Notch

Little People School Bus (Fisher-Price): A sturdy plastic yellow bus that's a fixture in most American playrooms. For good reason—kids adore it.

Little People Animal Sounds Farm (Fisher-Price): A great first play set.

Lego Duplo. Bigger than classic Lego, smaller than Duplo Primo. Get a basic set—perhaps contained in a small Duplo table.

The "Ooh, Ahh!" Gifts

Calin Baby Doll (Corolle): The ultimate baby doll—soft, lifelike, and her head even smells like vanilla.

Kid-size kitchen (Little Tikes): Girls *and* boys absolutely adore mini kitchens. This one is a goody. If you think parents will get bent out of shape if you give it to their macho little one, buy him a chunky plastic tool bench (Fisher-Price, Little Tikes, etc.). Girls actually love the latter, as well.

Classic red tricycle (Radio Flyer): The name says it all.

Rocking horse: Go for something classic in wood or in plastic—kids love them.

BOOKS: *Chicka Chicka Boom Boom;* DK's *My First Word Book; Are You My Mother?; Guess How Much I Love You; Brown Bear, Brown Bear, What Do You See?; Bark, George; Harold and the Purple Crayon.*

Third Birthday

WHAT'S DOING: This is the age when kids finally begin to realize that other children aren't merely something to bite, bump into, or bop over the head. They're actually fun to play with. Tap into this civilized turn of events by seeking out toys that encourage cooperative and dramatic play. A longer attention span makes this a perfect time to introduce basic craft materials.

WHAT THEY LIKE: Think dress-up outfits, doctors kits, play figures, balls, and puppets. Craft-wise, look for nontoxic molding clay, Play-Doh, and washable paints. Favorite books at this age are those that help kids explore various aspects of the world around them—farm animals, the seashore, transportation, and so on. Pop-up books help keep more active children interested.

Your Basic Great Gifts

Rescue Heroes (Fisher-Price): These rugged plastic action figures, which range from firefighters to helicopter pilots, look aggressive enough to interest rough-and-tumble little boys. What's nice is that they aren't out to kill or maim anyone—they're rescue heroes, get it?

Pretend tea or dish set (Alex, Battat): Look for sturdy, colorful plastic. Even if a child has a tea set already, she can always use extra settings.

Pretend dog or kitty carrier (widely available, any brand that looks good): A plastic pet carrier, often with a plush pet and grooming or vet accessories included.

Floor puzzles (Great American Puzzle Factory makes nice, sturdy ones): A sure bet for children this age—between twenty and forty pieces is about right.

Portable doctor's kit: Any brand that looks good. Fisher-Price's is a classic.

Taking It Up a Notch

Magna Doodle (Fisher-Price): The classic portable doodling board—kids draw and stamp away with a magnetic pen and stamps, then swipe it clean with the eraser bar and start again.

Grow-to-Pro Baseball (Fisher-Price): The set comes with lightweight plastic balls, a bat, a T, and an automatic pitcher that pops out five balls and makes batting practice a breeze.

Playmobil 1.2.3: Bigger chunkier pieces than traditional Playmobil, and a whole lot less of them to keep track of. Choose from a zillion sets geared for boys, girls, or both.

The "Ooh, Ahh!" Gifts

Thomas the Tank Engine Starter train set (Learning Curve): Lay the foundation for a wooden train set that will stay in play and be added onto through the years, and through the siblings. Brio also makes a nice—and slightly less expensive—wooden train set.

Wooden or plastic easel (Little Tikes, Alex, also log onto www.dickblick.com for a wide variety of fine children's easels): Two sides makes these fantastic for playdates as well as independent play.

Wooden unit block set (Constructive Playthings): Now's the time for those classic wooden building blocks. Don't skimp on chintzy lightweights—go for the pricier hardwoods and stick with basic shapes.

BOOKS: *Where the Wild Things Are; If You Give a Moose a Muffin* and other *If You Give . . .* books; *The Very Quiet Cricket* and other *Very* books by Eric Carle; *Make Way for Ducklings; The Cat in the Hat* and other Dr. Seuss beginner books; *Go, Dog. Go!; Harry the Dirty Dog* and other *Harry* books; *Cloudy With a Chance of Meatballs.*

Fourth Birthday

WHAT'S DOING: Four-year-olds are big on expressing themselves, through elaborate pretend play and via paint and paper.

WHAT THEY LOVE: Look for realistic, scaled-down versions of the things mom and dad use, plus toys and tools that will help a child explore the world around her, such as a magnifying glass or bug catcher. Dress-up clothes continue to thrill. This is the age for first board games that require only luck to play, such as Candy Land. Kids this age are ready to handle books with more involved story lines.

Your Basic Great Gifts

Woodkins play sets: A cool twist on the paper doll concept. A clear plastic carry case holds a wooden doll-shaped cutout, plus interchangeable faces and lots of clothes to mix and match.

Die-cast miniature cars, planes, trucks (Matchbox, Hot Wheels, and knock-offs): Don't bother with the fancy play sets and raceways they try to sell along with the vehicles. Just buy a big box full of cool vehicles—it will put any boy this age on Cloud Nine. Throw in a plastic carrying case if you want to get fancy.

Barbie clothes and accessories (Mattel): If you know the birthday girl has the green light on Barbie, assume she already has twelve of them. Give the dolls something to wear or somewhere to sit. Think clothes, cars, etc.

Taking It Up a Notch

Feltkids play sets (Learning Curve): Felt cutouts stick right onto a felt board—it's kind of like low-tech clip art. The travel play set is extra nice because it comes with a carrying case, a folding fabric play surface, and cutouts with a travel theme.

Ravensburger Snails Pace Race game (International Playthings): A welcome break from Candy Land and Chutes and Ladders.

Beefy metal toy trucks (Nylint): You can't lose here—cement mixers and dump trucks to RVs and awesome firetrucks.

Child-size umbrella: Schylling makes some colorful cuties. Also check museum gift shops; department store children's departments; and search online under "children's rainwear."

The "Ooh, Ahh!" Gifts

Pretend & Play Calculator Cash Register (Learning Resources): The price seems steep for a cash register, but this is the best of the lot. It operates primarily on solar energy, lasts for years, and comes packed with bills and change.

Plan Toys Wooden Dollhouse (Small World Toys): The pale wood and clean lines make this look a little dull compared to Barbie's florid pink palace. Trust us—it'll get lots more use and does more for the imagination.

BOOKS: *Olivia* books; *Madeline* books; *The Wonderful Happens; Something from Nothing; Anansi the Spider; Mike Mulligan and His Steam Shovel; The Velveteen Rabbit; Blueberries for Sal; Absolutely Positively Alexander.*

Fifth Birthday

WHAT'S DOING: At five, kids really start developing specific interests. One month, it might be planets and space, next a little expert may move on to professional baseball players. A child may also stick with something for a while—hopefully it will be something along the lines of meteorology or horses, as opposed to WWF icons.

WHAT THEY LOVE: Now is the time to tap into those interests. When you RSVP for a party, ask mom what her child is into these days. If he is into dinosaurs, add some minis to his collection. Girls start appreciating cool hats, gloves, and little purses. This is also the time to give jewelry boxes and decorative chests to hold hair clips and trinkets. Boys dig sports balls and equipment of all kinds. Also consider items that capitalize on a five-year-old's eagerness to take on responsibility and care for more "grown-up" gifts, such as a first wristwatch. This is also a good time for fairy-tale books that teach morals, poetry collections, as well as books for beginning readers.

Your Basic Great Gifts

Trouble (Milton Bradley): You remember, it's where you pop the bubble to spin the dice. Kids love it and parents who played the game as kids will be right back up to speed once they get a quick glance at the directions.

K'NEX Basic Building Set: Stay with the simple, open-ended stuff so mom and dad won't have to spend a week and a half studying the directions.

Child-size baseball/softball glove (Wilson): This is just about the time that T-ball starts. No problem if the gift is a repeat—at the rate children lose mitts, it's always nice to have an extra.

Alex Art Studio art supply kits (Alex): Colorful plastic carrying cases packed with all kinds of basic art stuff—paints, brushes, glue, rulers, markers, pencils. Perfect for travel.

Taking It Up a Notch

Lincoln Logs (Hasbro/K'NEX): If a child's already into these, chances are she needs more. Spice things up with some of the simple, themed kits or just enhance the basics.

Lego Freestyle: Let other parents buy those Lego model sets with eensy weensy pieces and complicated instructions. You provide a bulk tub of the good, basic stuff that can make—or be added onto—just about anything. The host parents may very well weep with gratitude. The birthday boy or girl will be happy, too.

Crayola Light-Up Tracing Desk (Binney & Smith): A self-contained kit with tracing paper, stencils, colored pencils, and a light that makes for easy tracing.

The "Ooh, Ahh!" Gifts

Pipsqueak coloring book playhouse: Yes, these are basically fancy cardboard boxes with designs on them. But let the Girlfriends tell you, kids color them and play in them for years and these babies really stand up through all the action.

American Girl dolls: Now's just about the right time for these lavishly detailed and widely loved collectibles. If a girl has one or two dolls already, there's no shortage of accessories out there for you to choose from.

Backyard soccer goal (lots of brands at a range of prices; check sporting goods superstores—brick and mortar or online): In case you don't know this already, one goal is enough for backyard play.

BOOKS: *Frog and Toad Are Friends; Owl Moon; The Magic Locket* and other magic charm books by Elizabeth Koda-Callan; *Amelia Bedelia; Sylvester and the Magic Pebble; The Story of Ferdinand; The Lorax; Horton Hears a Who; The Absolutely Essential Eloise; Beneath a Blue Umbrella.*

Sixth Birthday

WHAT'S DOING: Getting more agile and coordinated by the day, six-year-olds love physical activity and the outdoors. Pretend play begins to incorporate specific themes, from princes and princesses to house to cops and robbers to astronauts. Sixes are getting comfortable with reading on their own, but it's still great to continue the story time ritual.

WHAT THEY LOVE: Kids this age love items that pick up on the themes they're interested in—say, an outer-space puzzle or a first cookbook. Little girls are lovin' inexpensive lockets, charm bracelets, and other glam accessories. As for read-aloud books, sixes can really get into a good children's novel, complete with chapters.

Your Basic Great Gifts

Nana Banana Classics coloring books: Ornate coloring books featuring classic tales like Peter Pan and the Nutcracker. Throw in a box of crayons or tin of colored pencils.

The Most Incredible Outrageous, Packed-to-the-Gills, Bulging-at-the-Seams Sticker Book You've Ever Seen (Klutz): The name says it all. Regardless of age, regardless how many they've gone through, kids adore this.

Giant Horseshoe Magnet Kit (or other magnet kits from Dowling Magnets): One big magnet and a ton of cool stuff to latch onto it.

Guess Who? (Milton Bradley): Simple but very entertaining elimination board game.

Taking It Up a Notch

Pretend Soup and Other Real Recipes cookbook: A charming start for beginner cooks. Recipes are super easy to follow with lots of visual cues. Important—they're also edible.

Backyard Baseball, Football, Soccer, etc. (Humongous Entertainment): Any pick from this hugely popular CD-ROM series is a winner. Dads dig it, too.

Child's lap harp/zither (Music Maker): Track these lovely wooden instruments down at specialty stores or online. Sheets of music slip under the keys and make it easy for children to play familiar tunes in a matter of minutes. Will not, in all likelihood, induce parental teeth grinding or migraines.

The "Ooh, Ahh!" Gifts

Globe: Choose a classic desktop globe from Rand McNally or, if you want to make things a little flashier, buy the Geosafari Talking Globe, Jr.

Beanbag chair (try Lands' End, and online under "beanbags"): They're back . . . and now they really keep their shape. Kid-size versions are smaller and flaunt a ton of fun patterns from tie-dye to teddy bears, plus an array of bright solids.

Child-size luggage set (Samsonite makes some sturdy, colorful sets): Pieces usually include a wheeled suitcase, a backpack, and a fanny pack.

BOOKS: *American Girls* books; *Where the Sidewalk Ends* and other Shel Silverstein poetry collections; Fandex Family Field Guides (presidents, states, composers, dogs, etc.); Lewis Carroll's *Alice's Adventures in Wonderland; Frederick's Fables: A Leo Lionni Treasury of Favorite Stories; The Wonderful Wizard of Oz; Magic School Bus* books; *Nate the Great* books; *Ramona the Pest* and other *Ramona* books; *Charlie and the Chocolate Factory; Stuart Little* and other E. B. White classics.

Seventh Birthday

WHAT'S DOING: At seven, children really begin to value their own company—in fact, it's not uncommon for a boy or girl this age to step away from the playground crowd for a time and pursue quieter, more focused activities, such as reading, collecting, magic, computers, and exploring nature. Reading is really on a roll now.

WHAT THEY LOVE: Model, magic, and science kits are much loved, as are action figures. I-can-read books with a central character who shares a child's age and interests are winners, too.

Your Basic Great Gifts

Alex Musical Jewelry Box: One of the simpler and more satisfying "crafts kits" out there. Comes with a built-in music box and twirling ballerina; girls get to decorate it with jewels, ribbons, pearls, and other gewgaws included in the set.

Concentric Circle Dart Board (Dowling Magnets): These darts really latch on . . . to the dartboard. Lightweight, easy to set up and play anywhere.

Mancala (Cardinal Games, various other companies): Not only is this simple, ancient game totally fun for kids and grown-ups, it's lovely to look at and touch. Even the cheapest versions tend to come with wood boards and glass playing beads.

Taking It Up a Notch

I Dig Dinosaurs excavation kits (Earth Lore Ltd.): Kids this age and up get the most out of these projects since they're patient enough and dextrous enough to do the work nearly all on their own. They can chip and brush and chip and brush, pull the bones from a crumbly block, then assemble their own dino model.

I Spy Memory Game (Briarpatch): With their agile cobweb-free brains, kids show up the adults when they play this board game version of the classic *I Spy* books.

The "Ooh, Ahh!" Gifts

Starter keyboard (Casio makes basic affordables): Nothing too fancy—just an electronic keyboard with a variety of tones and rhythm patterns. It'll give kids a feel for what it's like to tickle the keys and parents some time to save for the real ebony and ivory.

Walkie-talkies (Motorola and others): Not the cheap ones that never worked when we were kids. The brave new breed—also known as family radios—that have a reach of at least two miles. The birthday child will love 'em—so will his parents when they head out to the theme park with the kids.

BOOKS: *Little House on the Prairie* books; *Superfudge* and other Fudge books; *Pippi Longstocking* books; DK children's illustrated encyclopedias and dictionaries; Magic Tree House books; *The Secret Garden, American Girls, Captain Underpants, Bailey School Kids.*

Eighth Birthday

WHAT'S DOING: Eight is a breakthrough age: Kids are getting more coordinated and are becoming better readers by the minute. They're not yet completely embarrassed to be seen with their parents—that's coming soon. But they're ready to take on a whole lot of stuff alone and with their friends.

WHAT THEY LOVE: Art and writing supplies, challenging construction sets, and electronic games are just about right. Books with exciting story lines and far-out adventures can capture these kids' attention.

Your Basic Great Gifts

Pipe Cleaners Gone Crazy (and other way-out activity kits from Klutz): Comes with about seventy-five pipe cleaners and a book that wittily describes oodles of ways to have fun with them.

Trivial Pursuit Junior (Parker Brothers): How can you miss?

Rush Hour (Binary Arts): Completely addictive sliding block puzzle. Can't think of a better way to amuse kids on long car trips.

Taking It Up a Notch

Anatomy Lab (Smithsonian): A human male figure with ten removable, anatomically detailed parts. (We know what you're wondering and the answer is "no.")

Deluxe Carpentry Tool Set (Popular Mechanics for Kids, or The Home Depot brand—sold at Toys "Я" Us): No plastic saws and hammers here—this is the real thing. Might want to check with mom first.

First diary, address book, or photo album: Stop by the book or paper supply store and let your child pick something out for her friend.

The "Ooh, Ahh!" Gifts

K'NEX contruction set: Go ahead, get one of the complicated motorized ones. At this point, the birthday child can show her mother how to use it.

Real jewelry: This might be the time for that first gold locket or sterling charm bracelet.

Basketball hoop and backboard (report directly to The Sports Authority or another real sporting goods store): That's right, Little Tikes won't cut it anymore. It's time for the real thing—before you know it you'll be dealing with athlete's foot, smelly socks, and B.O.

Tickets or a special day: Take a child you love to see *The Nutcracker* or to a major league game. Go for high tea or lunch at a fancy, frilly restaurant. Head off on a weekend camping trip. When all is said and done, experience is the "stuff" that ultimately makes life, particularly childhood, most meaningful.

BOOKS: *Harriet the Spy;* The Chronicles of Narnia; Time Warp Trio books; *A Wrinkle in Time; From the Mixed-up Files of Mrs. Basil E. Frankweiler; Little Women;* Nancy Drew mysteries; *The Last of the Really Great Whangdoodles; Where the Red Fern Grows; The Phantom Tollbooth; The Oxford Children's Book of Science.*

Top Ten Best Things About
Playing with Your Kids

10. Your little darling asks you which President "Richard Stands" was. When you ask why, she recites, "And to the Republic, of Richard Stands, one nation, under God . . ."

9. They truly believe you when you say some angels can float on big, white puffy clouds.

8. They still like you more than they like their friends (until about age ten).

7. They look forward to playdates and parties, truly.

6. You can eavesdrop on a playdate and hear one child say to the other, "Don't you love to powder the baby? Isn't she just precious?"

5. Everybody loves boxed juices. No big deal about caf and decaf.

4. No matter what happens, the kids are over it within an hour.

3. You cry every time the Birthday Song is sung to a child of your loins.

2. Within two or three hours, everyone will go home and you can go back to being your regular distracted self.

1. When your child is ecstatic, it's like angels are dancing on your shoulders. That's why we're willing to walk through this minefield again and again.

Some Reassuring Parting Remarks

Remember the day your brand-new baby was placed in your arms for the first time? You were sure you'd celebrate his or her birth every single day of the year and twice on Sundays. Well, it turns out that keeping that merriment going every single day, year after year, is actually a bigger challenge than you could ever have imagined. It's not that the joy isn't there; it's just that strangers get caught up in your mix. If life were truly a cabaret, ol' chum, then we'd never have to deal with finicky mothers, party no-shows, lost invitations, aggressive behavior, or being in the "out" crowd at the age of four.

Our best advice to you is this: You are not your child. Your child is not responsible for living up to your gregarious reputation or for making up for your wallflower memories. You know as well as we do that 99 percent of this childhood personality assessment will be absolutely meaningless by the time they hit high school (okay, maybe college). Bill Gates is the most attractive introvert on the planet and Anna-Nicole Smith may be friendly, but she's also antithetical to what we'd want our daughters to be. You have to love and accept that unique individual who is your darling babe and support him or her. Think what the world would have been like if Mrs. Spielberg had insisted that Steven go out for football instead of buying him a Super 8 camera.

Parties and playdates are just days to circle on the calendar, for you and your child to look forward to, to reminisce about, and to promise never to repeat. Your little one will make friends with or without your help, he'll learn to do the Macarena with or without professional instruction and he will be promoted into the great world of "big kids" whether you're ready or not. Try to make as many lovely memories as you can, thank Heaven for the gift of your child in your life, and remember, you will have a long life after these fleeting playing and partying years—save the treads on your maternal tires for the long run. Have fun!

Index

Index

Index

Index

Index

About the Authors

Vicki Iovine, a mother of four, lives with her family in southern California. She is also the author of *The Girlfriends' Guide to Pregnancy, The Girlfriends' Guide to Surviving the First Year of Motherhood, The Girlfriends' Guide to Toddlers, The Girlfriends' Guide to Getting Your Groove Back,* and *The Girlfriends' Guide to Baby Gear.* Visit Vicki Iovine online at www.girlfriendsguide.com.

Peg Rosen writes about health and family for numerous parenting and women's service publications. She has been on the staff
of *Bride's* magazine and most recently *Child*, where she was a
senior editor in charge of new products, prenatal health, and
early childhood development. A Certified Child Passenger Safety
Technician, Ms. Rosen writes and lectures often to parents about
car seat safety. She lives and works in Montclair, New Jersey, with
her husband, Paul Freundlich, and sons, Ben and Noah.